OBJECT-ORIENTED
ANALYSIS

BAUDIN Manufacturing Systems Analysis with Application to Production Scheduling
BELLIN AND SUCHMAN Structured Systems Development Manual
BLOCK The Politics of Projects
BODDIE Crunch Mode: Building Effective Systems on a Tight Schedule
BOULDIN Agents of Change: Managing the Introduction of Automated Tools
BRILL Building Controls into Structured Systems
BRILL Techniques of EDP Project Management: A Book of Readings
CHANG Principles of Visual Programming Systems
COAD AND YOURDON Object-Oriented Analysis
CONNELL AND SHAFER Structured Rapid Prototyping: An Evolutionary Approach to Software
   Development
CONSTANTINE AND YOURDON Structured Design: Fundamentals of a Discipline of Computer Program
   and Systems Design
DeMARCO Concise Notes on Software Engineering
DeMARCO Controlling Software Projects: Management, Measurement, and Estimates
DeMARCO Structured Analysis and System Specification
DeSALVO AND LIEBOWITZ Managing Artifical Intelligence and Expert Systems
DICKINSON Developing Structured Systems: A Methodology Using Structured Techniques
FLAVIN Fundamental Concepts in Information Modeling
FOLLMAN Business Applications with Microcomputers: A Guidebook for Building Your Own System
FRANTZEN AND McEVOY A Game Plan for Systems Development: Strategy and Steps for Designing Your
   Own System
INMON Information Engineering for the Practioner: Putting Theory into Practice
KELLER Expert Systems Technology: Development and Application
KELLER The Practice of Structured Analysis: Exploding Myths
KING Creating Effective Software: Computer Program Design Using the Jackson Method
KING Current Practices in Software Development: A Guide to Successful Systems
LIEBOWITZ AND DeSALVO Structuring Expert Systems: Domain, Design, and Development
McMENAMIN AND PALMER Essential System Analysis
ORR Structured Systems Development
PAGE-JONES Practical Guide to Structured Systems Design, 2/E
PETERS Software Design: Methods and Techniques
RIPPS An Implementation Guide to Real-Time Programming
RODGERS UNIX Database Management Systems
RUHL The Programmer's Survival Guide: Career Strategies for Computer Professionals
SCHMITT The OS/2 Programming Environment
SCHLAER AND MELLOR Object-Oriented Systems Analysis: Modeling the World in Data
THOMSETT People and Project Management
TOIGO Disaster Recovery Planning: Managing Risk and Catastrophe in Information Systems
VESELY Strategic Data Management: The Key to Corporate Competitiveness
WARD Systems Development Without Pain: A User's Guide to Modeling Organizational Patterns
WARD AND MELLOR Structured Development for Real-Time Systems, Volumes I, II, and III
WEAVER Using the Structured Techniques: A Case Study
WEINBERG Structured Analysis
YOURDON Classics in Software Engineering
YOURDON Managing the Structured Techniques, 4/E
YOURDON Managing the System Life Cycle, 2/E
YOURDON Modern Structured Analysis
YOURDON Structured Walkthroughs, 4/E
YOURDON Techniques of Program Structure and Design
YOURDON Writing of the Revolution: Selected Readings on Software Engineering

OBJECT-ORIENTED ANALYSIS

PETER COAD   EDWARD YOURDON

YOURDON Press
PRENTICE HALL, Englewood Cliffs, New Jersey 07632

Library of Congress Cataloging-in-Publication Data

COAD, PETER.
   Object-oriented analysis / Peter Coad, Edward Yourdon.

     p. cm.—(Yourdon Press Computing Series)
   Bibliography:
   Includes index.
   ISBN 0-13-629122-8
   1. System analysis. I. Yourdon, Edward. II. Title.
T57.6.C62 1990
620'.001'1—dc20   89-16028
                                  CIP

Editorial/production supervision: BARBARA MARTTINE
Cover design: WANDA LUBELSKA
Manufacturing buyer: PETER HAVENS

Published by Prentice-Hall, Inc.
A Division of Simon & Schuster
Englewood Cliffs, New Jersey 07632

The publisher offers discounts on this book when ordered
in bulk quantities. For more information, write:

        Special Sales/College Marketing
        College Technical and Reference Division
        Prentice Hall
        Englewood Cliffs, New Jersey 07632

Printed in the United States of America

10 9 8 7 6 5 4 3 2 1

ISBN   0-13-629122-8

TAB BOOKS Inc. offers software for sale. For information and a catalog, please contact
TAB Software Department, Blue Ridge Summit, PA 17294-0850.

PRENTICE-HALL INTERNATIONAL (UK) LIMITED, *London*
PRENTICE-HALL OF AUSTRALIA PTY. LIMITED, *Sydney*
PRENTICE-HALL CANADA INC., *Toronto*
PRENTICE-HALL HISPANOAMERICANA, S.A., *Mexico*
PRENTICE-HALL OF INDIA PRIVATE LIMITED, *New Delhi*
PRENTICE-HALL OF JAPAN, INC., *Tokyo*
SIMON & SCHUSTER ASIA PTE. LTD., *Singapore*
EDITORA PRENTICE-HALL DO BRASIL, LTDA., *Rio de Janeiro*

DEDICATION

To Judy, my best friend—this achievement is ours.

PC

To the editors, proofreaders, artists, printers, and myriad others behind the scenes without whose quiet, patient efforts a book like this would never see the light of day.

EY

CONTENTS

ACKNOWLEDGMENTS

From Pete Coad:

First, special thanks to two extraordinary teachers—ones who have instilled a passion for excellent teaching within me—the Drs. Mr. and Mrs. Peter Coad Sr. (Hi, Mom and Dad!).

Thank you to my clients and seminar participants in the U.S., Canada, Great Britain, West Germany, Israel, Italy, Sweden, and Australia. So much of what OOA is today is a direct result of your thoughtful considerations and suggestions. I remain most grateful.

Also, thank you to Mark Mitchell; Larry Young (Technology Training Corp.); Tammy Rimmer (JPL); Tom Jensen, Karen Reynolds (Hughes Aircraft Co.); Lin Conger (Mavelin Corp.); Howard Metcalfe, Dick Brewer, Bruce Eckoff, Penny Bevier (Telos Corp.); Bob Braden, Sandy Barling (Texas Dept. of Motor Vehicles); and Ralph Kirkley (Ralph Kirkley Associates).

From Ed Yourdon:

Thanks to a number of people who have urged me during the past several years to focus more on an object-oriented view of the world: Dave Bulman, Mike Silves, Larry Proctor, Steve and Greta Blash, and the late Matt Flavin. Thanks also to a group of authors whose work in the field over the past decade has helped lay a foundation for our work in this book: Grady Booch, Brad Cox, Bertrand Meyer, Adele Goldberg, Michael Jackson, Chris Gane, Ed Berard, and Ken Orr.

From both of us:

Thanks to the official reviewers of this manuscript, for their patient readings and valuable insights: Sam Adams (Knowledge Systems Corporation), Alan Davis (George Mason University), Tom Jensen (Hughes Aircraft Company), Charles McKay (University of Houston, Clear Lake), Michael Rissman (Software Engineering Institute), and Ed Seidewitz (Goddard Space Flight Center).

Thanks to Toni for her cheerful editing work... And thanks to the Prentice Hall staff that worked so diligently with us in producing this book, including Bernard Goodwin, Paul Becker, Barbara Marttine, and Noreen Regina.

OBJECT-ORIENTED ANALYSIS

0 INTRODUCTION

OOA—Object-Oriented Analysis—is based upon concepts that we first learned in kindergarten: objects and attributes, classes and members, wholes and parts. Why it has taken us so long to apply these concepts to the analysis and specification of information systems is anyone's guess—perhaps we've been too busy "following the flow" during the heyday of structured analysis to consider the alternatives.

As the Encyclopedia Britannica points out:

In apprehending the real world, men [people] constantly employ three methods of organization, which pervade all of their thinking:

(1) the differentiation of experience into particular objects and their attributes—e.g., when they distinguish between a tree and its size or spatial relations to other objects,

(2) the distinction between whole objects and their component parts—e.g., when they contrast a tree with its component branches, and

(3) the formation of and the distinction between different classes of objects—e.g., when they form the class of all trees and the class of all stones and distinguish between them.

Encyclopedia Britannica, "Classification Theory"

The notation and approach of OOA builds upon these three constantly employed methods of organization.

In 1984, one of the authors consulted, during a two and one-half year period, on the practical application of Real-Time Structured Analysis at a major aerospace company. His observations were interesting and yet disturbing. One team of analysts he studied (the "DFD Team") started their projects using data flow diagrams to develop an overall functional decomposition, as a framework for further specification. Meanwhile, a second team of analysts (the "Data Base Team") started by focusing on the information the system needed to do its job and then building an information model (also known as an Entity-Relationship Diagram or a Semantic Data Model). Over time, the DFD Team continued to struggle with the basic problem of space understanding (e.g., the details of what happens when one controller hands off responsibility for an aircraft to another controller). In contrast, the Data Base Team gained a strong, in-depth understanding of air traffic control. Yet the results did not mesh together; worse, they contradicted each other. In principle, these two models should somehow come together. Yet under the pressures of schedule and budget, both products moved unresolved into preliminary design, with the hope of resolving the discrepancies at that time. Sadly, the Data Base Team was perceived as irksome, even somewhat as troublemakers; people (and their careers) paid the price for this major rift and its untidy resolution.

In 1987 and 1988, the same author saw this same pattern develop on projects at a federal government agency and a state government agency. The DFD Team marched on, ahead in time and political power. The Data Base team gained tremendous insight, vital to analysis but all too-often ignored. And again, the Data Base Teams and their leaders were perceived as troublemakers.

Repeatedly, *in practice,* separate notations and strategies for different process and data models have kept the two forever apart. Because of this chasm, we began the research and development of method—notations and strategies—that would help analysts gain the much-needed problem space understanding first, and then add the processing requirements within the framework of that solid understanding. We put the method to work in practice, refining and building the approach into a systematic method. Finally, one of the authors presented the method to top professionals throughout the United States, plus Canada, Israel, Italy, the Federal Republic of Germany, Sweden, and the United Kingdom, receiving valuable feedback and insight from the participants. In applying OOA on actual projects, both clients and seminar participants significantly contributed to the development of this method.

0.1 ORGANIZATION

This book, which we believe is the first of its kind, presents OOA in nine chapters.

Chapters 1 and 2 lay the foundation. "Improving Analysis" examines the challenge of systems analysis, and then reviews some principles for managing complexity. It then summarizes four popular analysis methods: Functional Decomposition, Data Flow, Information Modeling, and Object-Oriented. Chapter 2, "Experiencing An Object Perspective," explores a fully object-oriented programming language and environment to illustrate some key points for use in OOA.

Chapters 3 through 7 cover the OOA method in five major steps: Identifying Objects, Identifying Structure, Defining Attributes, Defining Connections, and Defining Services. Each chapter is organized into What, Why, How to Define, and Key Points (a concise summary).

Chapter 8, "Selecting CASE for OOA," describes Computer-Aided Software Engineering (CASE) support for OOA, showing what is needed and what is currently available.

Finally, Chapter 9 moves into Object-Oriented Design (OOD), describing design considerations, and what happens to the OOA model as OOD proceeds.

An appendix, "Mapping OOA to DOD-STD-2167A," illustrates how to apply OOA when working under the U.S. Defense Department's DOD-STD-2167A, *Defense System Software Development.*

0.2 WHY DO WE NEED OOA?

Seven prime reasons underlie the logic of using OOA:

1. It allows us to define and communicate the requirements of a system within the framework of

the *three basic methods of human organization* (Object and Attributes, Classification Structure, and Assembly Structure).

2.　It focuses primarily on *problem space understanding*—an understanding of the world and application domain the user lives in, and the nature of the system he wants to automate.

3.　It treats object Attributes and exclusive Services on those Attributes as an *intrinsic whole*, in contrast to other analysis methods which deal with these issues separately or incompletely. Thus, it combines the data and process model into one complete model.

4.　It allows us to analyze and specify systems using *self-contained* partitioning (minimal dependency between one object and others). This leads to a more stable model.

5.　It allows us to gain leverage through *explicit representation of commonality*.

6.　It applies a *consistent, powerful underlying representation* for analysis (what is to be built) and design (how it is to be built this time).

7.　It allows us to accommodate *families* of systems, and to accommodate ongoing practical tradeoffs—e.g., a full system versus a system with fewer implemented features.

0.3 AUDIENCE

We have aimed this book at the practicing systems analyst, the person who has to tackle real-world systems development projects every day. We assume a fundamental understanding of computer technology and systems analysis concepts, and we expect that many of our readers will have had some experience with such analysis tools as data flow diagrams and entity relationship diagrams. Managers, testers, standards bearers, and users can read the book and expect to profit from the overall approach to improving systems analysis.

0.4 FOCUS AND HISTORY

Though it will become abundantly clear in the following chapters, we should stress here that our concern in this book is with object-oriented *analysis*, not Object-Oriented Programming (OOP) or Object-Oriented Design (OOD). Systems analysts first must understand the problem domain at hand; it makes little sense to run off and start writing air traffic control functional requirements—let alone thinking about design architectures or writing code—without first studying, expressing, and validating our understanding of what air traffic control is really all about. Objects as abstractions of the real world provide a focus on gaining significant problem space understanding; ultimately this knowledge results in a tangible, reviewable, and manageable collection of model layers (Subject, Object, Structure, Attribute, Connection, and Service) produced during the five major steps of OOA.

We could argue that this perspective has *always* been important, even if it has not been a terribly popular one. If this case is true, then why this book on OOA? Why has the "object paradigm" finally come of age? Why now?

Object-oriented *programming* was first discussed in the late 1960s by those working with the SIMULA language. By the 1970s, it was an important part of the Smalltalk language developed at Xerox PARC. Meanwhile, the rest of the world bumbled along with languages like COBOL and FORTRAN, and used functional decomposition methods (which we will discuss in more detail in Chapter 1) to address problems of design and specification. Little, if any, discussion focused on object-oriented *design*, and virtually none on object-oriented *analysis*.

Four changes have occurred over the past decade, and are now key factors as we enter the 1990s:

- The underlying concepts of an object-oriented approach have had a decade to mature, and attention has gradually shifted from issues of coding, to issues of design, to issues of analysis. The proponents of functional decomposition spent a decade progressing from structured programming to structured design to structured analysis; we should not be surprised to see the same progression in the object-oriented world.

- The underlying technology for building systems has become much more powerful. Unfortunately, our way of thinking about systems analysis is influenced by our preconceived ideas of how we would design a system to meet its requirements; our ideas about design are influenced by our preconceived ideas about how we would write code; and our ideas about coding are strongly influenced by the programming language we have available. It was difficult to think about structured programming (and thus difficult to think about structured design and analysis) when the languages of choice were assembler, AUTOCODER and FORTRAN; things became easier with PASCAL, PL/1, ALGOL, FORTRAN-77, Structured BASIC, and newer versions of COBOL. Similarly, it was difficult to think about coding in an object-oriented fashion when the language of choice was COBOL, FORTRAN, or plain-vanilla C; it has become easier with C++, Objective-C, Smalltalk, and Ada.

- The systems we build today are different than they were ten or twenty years ago. In every respect, they are larger and more complex; they are also more volatile and subject to constant change. We will argue in subsequent chapters that an object-oriented approach to analysis (and design) is likely to lead to a more stable system. Also, we find that today's on-line, interactive systems devote much more attention to the *user interface* than the text-oriented batch processing systems of the 1960s and 1970s. Some observers, such as Bill Joy of Sun Microsystems, argue that as much as 75 percent of the code in a modern system may be concerned with the user interface—e.g., manipulating windows, pull-down menus, icons, mouse movements, etc. Our experience has been that an object-oriented approach to such systems—from analysis through design and into coding—is a more natural way of dealing with such user-oriented systems.

• Many organizations find that the systems they build today are more "data-oriented" than the systems they built in the 1970s and 1980s. Functional complexity is less of a concern than it was before; modeling the data has become a higher priority.

0.5 FUTURE ADVANCES IN OOA

OOA is a relatively young method; it will continue to evolve in practice. So we implore you, the reader, not to come up to us at computer conferences and say that you are developing software "compliant with the Coad/Yourdon OOA standard." Rather, use this book as a starting point for applying OOA—tailoring and expanding the method to suit your specific organization or project needs.

To provide you with periodic updates on OOA, a business reply card offering free special reports, *The Coad Letter: New Advances in OOA*, is included with this book. Send the card to Peter Coad at Object International, Inc., 3202 W. Anderson, Suite 208-724, Austin TX 78757, USA.

We expect to further develop OOA over time. Some of the issues under consideration include the following:

1. Using OOA to describe OOA itself.

2. Adding explicit parameters for all messages that invoke non-implicit Services.

3.   Adding messages that do not require a response.

4.   Allowing Attributes to be Objects themselves, weighing the advantages of nested Objects against the disadvantages of a perceived increase of complexity.

5.   Adding specific guidelines for risk identification, analysis, and management for Object-Oriented Development.

6.   Investigating OOA and OOD as two views of a complete solution.

7.   Adding and distinguishing between Objects and Collections of Objects.

1 IMPROVING ANALYSIS

1.1 THE ANALYSIS CHALLENGE

Systems analysis exhilarates and aggravates those who fall prey
to its siren song. What is so difficult about analysis? What is
the challenge? We feel three major difficulties plague systems
analysts on all types of projects: problem space understanding,
person-to-person communication, and continual change.

1.1.1 The Problem Space

One of the biggest problems faced by analysts is studying the
application domain and making discoveries about it. It's the
challenge of understanding the "problem space."   As
consultants, we usually experienced this problem in an
extreme form: we were dropped into a project for a week, a
month, or occasionally as long as a year. In most cases, we
couldn't pretend at all to be a subject matter expert in the
client's business or application. We needed to grasp, to
understand in depth, the problem space—and we needed to
do it as quickly as possible. Of course, the situation is less
extreme for many systems analysts—but even if you happen to
be such a subject matter expert as well as an analyst, you still
need tools to effectively communicate your expertise to others
on your team. For example, if you have been working with
radar systems for the past 20 years, you probably have intimate
knowledge of the problem space; if the time has come to
specify the requirements for yet another radar system, your
primary problem may be that of communicating with other
radar experts as well as project members who can't
distinguish a radar from a grapefruit.

Analysts must consider the problem space in which they work. For example, consider the problem of air traffic control. The analyst needs to immerse himself in that problem space, immerse himself so deeply that he begins to discover nuances that even those who live with air traffic control every day have not yet fully considered. As another example, consider a business system that maintains information about automobile registrations and titles; an analyst working on such a system would need to study and assimilate all sorts of details—and many exceptions to the rules, resulting from special interest group demands and the statutes that follow.

This discussion has described a major part of what it's all about to be an effective analyst. It's much more than just writing some observable, measurable functional requirements. Yes, an analyst needs to specify processing requirements, concisely packaged so that fellow human beings can read and understand what he believes those requirements are. But understanding the problem space is really the crux of systems analysis.

If an analyst simply assumes that he has subject matter knowledge, he is likely to indulge in thinking that will lead to fuzzy requirements. One of the authors was recently involved in a large air traffic control project, in which requirements analysts were still grappling with basic air traffic control concepts even after two years of specifying software requirements. This situation should not have occurred. Analysts need to understand and model the problem space, *especially* for large, complex systems; with such understanding, the textual specifying of measurable requirements can be done in a fairly straightforward fashion.[1]

---

[1] Regardless of the methodology or modeling approach, it is unlikely that an analyst will fully understand the problem space at the beginning of a project. Analysis is a process of continual learning about the subject matter and its nuances.

1.1.2   Communication

The analysis challenge also requires communication. An analyst needs to communicate throughout the analysis effort. He must communicate just to extract the problem space and requirements from the client. He thinks about all of this communication and refines it himself. He interacts with his peers.   Ultimately, he needs to echo his problem space understanding and subsequent requirements back to the client, to validate his understanding of the requirements. He may also need help in steering his client away from requirements that cannot be met within budget and schedule constraints.

A funny irony exists in the term "software engineering": though the words conjure up images of formulas, algorithms, and "hard" scientific approaches, software engineering is actually a very people-oriented business. Recently, one of the authors spoke at a conference in Chicago and was asked if OOA (and/or other software methods) was the key to successful software development.   The response?   Yes, having a consistent technical approach is very valuable. Yet software methods are effective only to the extent that they help people to communicate with one another. If the application of a software engineering "method" produces a monument of paper, then something is wrong—in the method, in the application of the method, or perhaps both. If we lose sight of people and begin producing charts, diagrams, and piles of paper as an end unto itself, we fail to effectively communicate. Software engineering is a people business. People make the problems; people solve the problems. And we can solve our systems development problems only by interacting with each other.

At this same computer conference, the beleaguered author then did a "bad" thing. He asked how many educators in the audience required some interpersonal communications training as part of their software engineering program. *No hands were raised.*   Yet effective communication—with management, peers, reviewers, standards bearers, and clients—is vital to successful systems analysis.

Viable software methods must facilitate communication. Successful software methods build upon human methods of organization, rather than upon a contrived notation that works well for computation (e.g., "follow the flow") but not for humans.

1.1.3   Continual Change

Requirements continue to be in a state of flux. Management or clients may impose an artificial freezing of requirements at a particular point in time. But the true requirements, the needed system, will continue to evolve. Many forces affect this ever-changing requirements set: customers, competition, regulators, approvers, and technologists. As Gerhard Fischer [Fischer, 1989] points out, "We have to accept changing requirements as a fact of life, and not condemn them as a product of sloppy thinking."

An analyst endeavors to organize his notations and strategies so that his work is resilient to change. He seeks requirements packaging that will remain stable over time. The explicit capture of commonality is a great help here, for both data and processing. And as he finds computer implementation issues and other design considerations, he tucks them off into a file folder, deferring added complexity until the requirements are put forth.

1.2 MANAGING COMPLEXITY

This section sets forth the major principles underlying OOA.

1.2.1   Abstraction

The first principle is abstraction:

> Abstraction. The principle of ignoring those aspects of a subject that are not relevant to the current purpose in order to concentrate more fully on those that are. [Oxford, 1986]

This term means that even though an analyst knows about other things, he chooses certain things over others.

Both authors have young sons whose rooms are filled with a variety of toys, many of which are small-scale replicas of airplanes, cars, and exotic warriors. It's interesting to see how even little children deal with the concept of abstraction: a little toy hook-and-ladder fire truck, for example, could have been built with a hundred pound hose hanging off its side. But the abstraction would be out of proportion, and rendered useless for its intended user. Yet we know, and even the child knows, that the hose is there; its complexity we need in the real system; but it would be inappropriate for the abstraction our children play with on their bedroom floors.

Most of what we deal with in the real world—people, places, objects, and systems—are intrinsically complex, far more complex than we can cope with in one fell swoop. When we use the concept of abstraction, we admit that what we are considering is complex; rather than try to comprehend the entire thing, we select only part of it. We know it contains additional details; we simply choose not to use them at this time. This technique is an important way to manage complexity.

Procedural abstraction is one form of abstraction used extensively by requirements analysts, as well as designers and programmers. It's often characterized as "function/sub-function" abstraction. You may be familiar with diagramming methods such as structure charts, with the big box at the top—representing the entire system, or "thing" being considered—and the subordinate steps or sub-functions shown as smaller boxes below the top-level box.

> Procedural Abstraction. The principle that any operation that achieves a well-defined effect can be treated by its users as a single entity, despite the fact that the operation may actually be achieved by some sequence of lower-level operations. [Oxford, 1986]

Breaking processing (e.g., aircraft tracking) down into sub-steps is one basic method of handling complexity. But, as we will discuss in more detail below, using such a breakdown for organizing analysis and specification is somewhat arbitrary and highly volatile. Procedural abstraction is not the primary form of abstraction for OOA; however, it does come into play in OOA within the limited context of specifying and describing individual Objects.

Another, more powerful abstraction mechanism is data abstraction. This principle is at the core of OOA. This principle forms the basis for the primary organization of thinking and specification.

> Data Abstraction. The principle of defining a data type in terms of the operations that apply to objects of the type, with the constraint that the values of such objects can be modified and observed only by the use of the operations. [Oxford, 1986]

In OOA, an analyst defines Attributes of Objects. And he defines Services that exclusively manipulate those Attributes.[2] The only way to get to the Attributes is via a Service. Attributes and their Services are treated as an intrinsic whole in the OOA approach. Indeed, note that Attributes, Objects, and Services are so important to the OOA approach that we capitalize the words whenever they are used throughout the book—i.e., Attribute, Object, Service.

1.2.2   Information Hiding (Encapsulation)

Another principle for managing complexity is information hiding:

> Information Hiding. A principle, used when developing an overall program structure, that each component of a program should encapsulate or hide a single design decision.... The interface to each module is defined in such a way as to reveal as little as possible about its inner workings. [Oxford, 1986]

This definition reflects the design work of David Parnas [Parnas, 1972] in the early 1970s.

The power and attractiveness of information hiding is that it helps minimize rework when developing a new system.

---

[2] For those familiar with other forms of systems analysis, the term "service" may be considered equivalent to "function" or "process."

If an analyst encapsulates the parts of the requirements analysis effort that are most volatile, then the (inevitable) changing of requirements becomes less of a threat to the overall effort. Localizing volatility is essential: whether we like it or not, we as analysts live in an environment of continual change. *Encapsulation is done to separate the user of an Object from its author.*

1.2.3   Inheritance

Inheritance is another underlying principle of OOA:

> Inheritance: Properties or characteristics received from an ancestor.

This principle forms the basis for a powerful technique of explicit expression of commonality, which we will discuss in further detail in Chapter 7. Inheritance allows us to specify common Attributes and Services *once,* as well as specialize and extend those Attributes and Services into specific cases. Thus, we might recognize automobiles and trucks as special cases in a transportation system: each of these special cases "inherits" common Attributes (e.g., Vehicle ID) of the generic Object "vehicle."

Using the concept of inheritance, a receiver (e.g., the Object known as "automobile") acquires properties— Attributes and Services—from a giver (e.g., the Object known as "vehicle"). In addition, the receiver can add to or extend those properties. Thus, the "truck" Object might have Attributes such as "number-of-axles" or "number-of-wheels," which might not be relevant or appropriate for the Object known as "automobile."

OOA uses inheritance to explicitly express commonality, beginning with the early activities of requirements analysis.

1.2.4   Methods of Organization

As authors, it would be intellectually satisfying if we could report that we studied the philosophical ideas behind methods of organization, from Aristotle and Socrates to Descartes and Kant. Then, based on the underlying methods human beings use, we could propose the basic constructs essential to a requirements analysis method, and in particular to OOA. But in truth, we cannot say that, nor did we do it.

However, we approached the problem as practitioners and investigators. We researched and applied various software subjects, in particular, semantic data modeling and object-oriented programming languages. We began to ferret out some of the embellishments, looking for the key principles that could be applied to organizing and representing requirements. We looked for the concepts that gave the greatest leverage in understanding and expressing problem space knowledge. And we boiled it down to three key methods of organization.

Though we cannot claim to have made a comprehensive survey of classification theory and the organizational methods proposed by philosophers and thinkers during the past three thousand years, we did check out Encyclopedia Britannica, to read about how people organize problem space. Here's what we found:

> In apprehending the real world, men [people] constantly employ three methods of organization, which pervade all of their thinking:
>
> (1) the differentiation of experience into particular objects and their attributes – e.g., when they distinguish between a tree and its size or spatial relations to other objects,
>
> (2) the distinction between whole objects and their component parts – e.g., when they contrast a tree with its component branches, and
>
> (3) the formation of and the distinction between different classes of objects – e.g., when they form the class of all trees and the class of all stones and distinguish between them.
>
> Encyclopedia Britannica, "Classification Theory"

The notation and approach of OOA is built upon these three constantly employed methods of organization. In OOA, they are referred to, respectively, as Objects and Attributes, Assembly Structures, and Classification Structures.

1.3 ANALYSIS METHODS

This section surveys four major approaches to requirements analysis. These approaches are thinking tools, used to help in the formulation of requirements.

First, what is systems analysis? DeMarco [DeMarco, 1978] offers the following definition: "Analysis is the study of a problem, prior to taking some action."

To us, analysis is the study of a problem space, leading to a specification of externally observable behavior—a complete, consistent, and feasible statement of what is needed.

Analysis means the process of extracting the "needs" of a system—*what* the system must do to satisfy the customer, not *how* the system will be implemented. Systems analysis usually begins with a textual requirements document, a series of discussions with a client, or both. In any case, the audience includes the end-user of the system, the developers of the system, and possibly other interested parties (e.g., auditors, contracting officers, etc.) who may need to understand and agree with the proposed set of requirements. The requirements document should communicate a complete, consistent, and feasible statement of what is needed in the system. It should be manageable both before and after it is produced. Requirements include functional operations and (quantified!) operational characteristics such as ease-of-use, reliability, availability, maintainability, and performance. Requirements also include interfaces that the software must deal with, environments the software must accommodate, and any other applicable design constraints.

A requirements document has two purposes: (1) it formalizes the needs of the customer, and (2) it establishes a list of mandates.

The first three approaches to requirements analysis have been discussed and practiced in the systems development profession for a decade or more. We have personally used all three methods on large systems, sometimes with successful results and sometimes with abject failure. The strengths of these first three methods have their place in specific contexts in the fourth method discussed in this section, OOA. Thus, we feel it is important to emphasize that we are not trying to abolish the older, more established methods—that would be akin to throwing the baby out with the bath water. Software methods should be utterly pragmatic, without religious fervor. An analyst needs all the help he can get. What we are attempting to do is to incorporate the best ideas of the first three methods in a more comprehensive, all-encompassing method—OOA.

Rather than endlessly argue about which method is best, we prefer to take a pragmatic view, using whatever combination of approaches helps in a given situation, no matter which method it comes from.

Each approach is defined below with an equation, for easy recognition of the method. Each approach is also examined in light of large project experience.

1.3.1   Functional Decomposition

Functional decomposition is readily recognized with its steps and sub-steps. An equation representation, useful in identifying this method in use, is:

Functional Decomposition =
    Functions
    + Sub-functions
    + Functional interfaces.

This representation defines how we recognize that something has been functionally decomposed.

The underlying strategy of functional decomposition consists of selecting the processing steps and sub-steps anticipated for a new system, using previous experience as a guide. The focus is on *what processing* is required for the new system. The analyst then specifies the processing and functional interfaces.

Figure 1.1: *Functional Decomposition*

Functional decomposition requires humans to map from problem space (e.g., air traffic control) to functions and sub-functions. The analyst must internalize the subject matter, and then document the corresponding required functions and sub-functions that the system shall provide. The resulting specification only *indirectly* maps back to the subject matter.[3] Nothing explicitly maps the functionality back to the subject matter itself. This method makes it difficult for the analyst and the user to assess whether or not the requirements are an accurate statement of what the new system is required to do. With such an approach, problem space understanding is neither explicitly expressed nor verified for its accuracy; subtle distinctions within the problem space are simply not uncovered.

Is functional decomposition bad? No! After all, eventually both data and data processing must be specified. In fact, OOA uses functional decomposition (gasp!), albeit in a very specific context: defining certain Services (processing)

---

[3] The indirect mapping exists even if the client provides a list of requirements. The analyst must still understand the subject matter and verify it with the client before proceeding.

for a specific Object. In other words, it may be helpful to break up a large, complicated Service into smaller pieces for convenience in stating what is required. For example, for an "Aircraft" Object, an analyst will probably divide a description of the "Aircraft.Track" Service into a number of smaller pieces. He may also use a block diagram or data flow diagram fragment to help guide the reader through the requirements of this Service. But this definition is all done within the context of an Object; the processing steps are not used as the primary underlying representation during analysis or specification; processing steps are too volatile over time.

Function/sub-function breakdowns are difficult to construct (because of the indirect mapping) and highly volatile (because of the continual change of functional capability, which can be successfully delivered within budget and schedule constraints). For these reasons, we feel that the overall analysis approach should *not* be based on function/sub-function; a more stable analysis viewpoint and specification organization is needed.

In functional decomposition, analysts end up with system, sub-system, function, and sub-function levels. The problem lies in choosing the functions and knowing the change volatility of system functionality. Another problem facing the analyst is choosing the functions and sub-functions in such a way that the interface bandwidth is minimized, both now and over time. Though earlier textbooks (see, for example, [Yourdon and Constantine, 1979] and [Page-Jones, 1988]) used the concepts of *coupling* and *cohesion* to describe the composition of system components and the interfaces between those components, many system developers had a difficult time identifying sub-functions so that when a processing change came, they captured the new requirements with a minimum of change to the analysis and specification organization.

1.3.2   Data Flow Approach

Another method (and another way to map problem space into a technical representation) is the data flow approach, often described as "structured analysis." One can recognize a data flow approach with this equation:

Data Flow Approach =
    Data (& control) flows
    + Data (& control) transformations
    + Data (& control) stores
    + Terminators
    + Minispecs
    + Dictionary.

This notation is basic. Sometimes an information model (by various names, e.g., Entity-Relationship Diagrams) is used too; these models will be discussed later in this chapter.

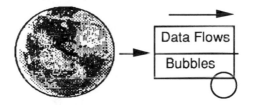

Figure 1.2: *Data Flow Decomposition*

With this method, the analyst maps from the real world into data flows and bubbles. This mapping requires the analyst (and more significantly, the customer) to follow the flow of data whenever looking at the real world, and map that flow into subsequent analysis and specification. Yet "follow the flow of data" is not one of the basic methods many humans use to manage complexity when looking at a problem space. In other words, it is not one of the basic methods of organization that pervade people's thinking. Considering an event (e.g., a transaction request) and then identifying the processing steps taken in response to that event is quite helpful, and is in fact one of the secondary strategies in OOA for identifying Services and the steps within a Service. But this flow describes processing steps (using procedural abstraction), not the flow of data and its gradual refinement (which is a thinking approach that leads to procedural abstraction).

Two major strategies predominate Structured Analysis. The "old" method (see [DeMarco, 1978] and [Gane and Sarson, 1977]) maps the current system to data flow diagrams, removes the physical idiosyncrasies, adds new logical requirements, and then adds new physical considerations.

For the current U.S. Air Traffic Control System, or for many states' registration and title systems, the documentation of end-user requirements of the existing system consisted of little more than source code and patched object code from the late 1960s. Studying and modeling such systems was, in effect, studying and modeling a prior mapping of the problem space, rather than the problem space itself. Analysts find it difficult to recover from this misplaced focus of study.

The problems with this older strategy became apparent as team after team got ensnared in trying to model the current system, while time, budget, and patience wore out. Analysts just did not know when to stop (and when in doubt, kept adding to the model). As our colleague Steve McMenamin observes, many analysts fell into the "current physical tarpit," never to emerge.

The "modern" approach first appeared in seminars as early as 1982, in books as early as 1984 (see, for example, [McMenamin and Palmer, 1984]), and more recently in Yourdon's *Modern Structured Analysis* in 1989 [Yourdon, 1989]. The strategy developed because analysts had problems picking bubbles for their data flow diagrams. So, to assist in picking the bubbles, the first step is to define events. Events are those occurrences that happen in the outside world that a planned-response system must respond to.[4]

---

[4] The actual interaction between the user and system is message-based. The event list documented in the "modern" approach to structured analysis is largely a documentation of the individual requests made by human users, so that the event+data flow correspondence can be expressed.

Each event corresponds to a bubble; for a system with 150 events, draw 150 bubbles. Name each bubble by deciding what the system does in response to the event. Add appropriate input and output flows to each bubble. Place data stores between bubbles that need to communicate with data held over time. Then, group the bubbles into page-size bites. Next, draw higher-level summaries, up two or three levels, the highest of which is a "context diagram" in which the entire system is shown as a single bubble. For lower-level bubbles, apply functional decomposition to define even lower levels, as needed.

The additional documentation needed includes specifying the data flows and bottom-level transformations with a data dictionary and process specifications, respectively. The upper level diagrams exist to provide a big picture for the reader; the process specification content expresses the detail. But much of the lower level detail must be understood for the graphical summaries to make much sense.

The challenge is in how to pick the bubbles. Event-response partitioning can help. But with too many events, the number of bubbles gets out of hand. And little help is given on making groups of higher levels to improve human understandability—the guideline of "group bubbles that deal with common data stores" sounds sensible, but often breaks down in practice. Far too often organizations fight "bubble wars" for extended periods of time, trying to decide which partitioning is the best choice. Eventually the upper level bubbles become such conglomerates that their names can say little more than "Process <noun>".

Another problem with the data flow method is the size of the data dictionary. If five levels of diagrams exist, hundreds of data flow leveling equations may be required. Moreover, complex interfaces (with other systems, devices, and humans) tend to aggravate the data dictionary equation problem, leading to project data dictionary "explosions" of 1000+ pages of dictionary documentation (the authors have seen a number of large projects with this recurring problem).

Using a message-based interaction model expresses the correspondence directly.

CASE tools can help get all the syntax in shape. But the semantics, the underlying meaning, is beyond what any human reviewer can digest. So communication, most vital in requirements analysis, is greatly weakened. Moreover, interfaces are volatile. The continual change for systems with complex interfaces only causes even further syntactic and (more significantly) semantic consistency problems.

The data flow approach still has a strong functional emphasis. And thus it is subject to the same change resiliency weaknesses that we discussed earlier.

The data flow approach has very weak data structure emphasis, and this is one of the greater concerns. The data flow diagram gives very weak emphasis to the data store. And this weakness is duly acknowledged by many authors describing the data flow method. So many authors have tried to tie information modeling concepts into data flow diagramming to compensate for the weakness. It's an academically pleasing idea (two perspectives, one system under consideration). Yet even in books, the connection is very weak—e.g., [Yourdon, 1989] discusses the tie in, but the leverage attainable in problem space understanding from data modeling and its influence on a data flow model is all but ignored. And, more important than what a textbook says, *in practice the connection seems virtually non-existent.* On large projects that we have observed at several defense contractors, as well as at a variety of business data processing organizations, the same pattern emerges again and again:

- The analysts rush off to do data flow diagrams.

- After a while, out of synch in time and content, another team works on an information model (this team is called the "database group").

- The second team gets great subject matter understanding.

- The first team likes the insight but resists the massive changes they must make (having grabbed for functionality first).

- The functional (DFD) team wins out, and the results of the two teams never get reconciled ("oh, we'll put it together in design").

Each analyst needs the benefit of both perspectives. *In practice, separate models keep critical issues too disjoint.* And although CASE tool support could help somewhat, the analyst with data flow diagrams works primarily with a model that hides the impact of the data structure. Seeing this need again and again spurred us on to develop a single, multiple-layered notation for OOA; analysts can see the layers they want to see within one model, with the ability to view Objects, Structures, Attributes, Connections, and Services as a unified whole.

Another concern follows. DFDs are not very helpful for systems or parts of systems that primarily update and retrieve data. Unlike the familiar transaction processing systems of the 1970s and early 1980s, this pattern appears in most real-world systems today: the diagrams basically show a pair of bubbles, one bubble getting data and writing into a store, and one bubble pulling information out of that store, delivering the data. For example, an air traffic control system for the most part uses a bubble to dump in the data, and another bubble to later retrieve the data. Most of the system can be specified in this fashion. Pretty bubble-to-bubble-to-bubble textbook transformations are limited to fairly small aspects of the system, in which the processing is extensive enough to warrant such a refinement of data from one sub-step to the next and so on—e.g., tracking calculations, where tracking is a very important but rather small part when compared to the overall system to be analyzed and specified.

Another major concern about the data flow approach is moving to design: the double burden of shifting underlying method of organization *and* adding implementation detail. This burden reminds the authors of the cartoon that shows a wide planning chart coming together at one point, with a box reading "and then a miracle happens," followed by a wide path of planning charts emanating from the box. The transition from analysis to design has been a constant source of aggravation. Many papers have been written; little progress has been made. It's tough enough to add implementation-based design considerations. Adding a substantial shift in underlying representation has made this transition such an untenable problem. Data flows are a network representation of bubbles and stores; design-oriented structure charts are a hierarchical representation of modules. And no matter how many cute cartoons are drawn to depict the transition, the radical change in underlying representation causes a major chasm between analysis and design models. As Seidewitz argues [Seidewitz, unpublished paper], "Functional analysis and specification techniques actually sacrifice closeness to the problem domain in order to allow a smooth transition to functional design methods."

A similar problem plagues those who have tried to follow structured analysis with object-oriented design; this trouble seems especially popular with those wrestling with Ada-oriented methods. However, if the object-oriented paradigm is so powerful as an underlying design perspective, why not apply those concepts as a foundation for improving requirements analysis? This technique seems far more natural than many of the 10-100 page papers we have seen on such a transition, which in effect say, "Oh good. The analysts have done their structured analysis stuff. Let's pick the pieces of their results to get a first-cut, object-oriented view. Then on to the good stuff—design." This change is even more drastic when underlying representation causes an even larger gap between analysis and design models. Such a gap is disastrous over time: requirements documents are ignored, continual changes in requirements are difficult to move into the design, and traceability—a must in Government system acquisition—is left with only form, and very little content.

For many years, analysts were stymied with the underlying representation shift as they moved from analysis to design. It prevented practitioners from systematically adding design-dependent detail to the results of requirements analysis. Design should consist solely of expanding the requirements model to account for the complexities introduced in selecting a particular implementation—e.g., multiple computational resources this time, particular display devices this time, added Objects to manage other Objects this time, and added Objects to manage external interfaces this time. Problem space Objects, such as Aircraft, continue from analysis into design.

It's a matter of using the same underlying representation in analysis and design. This concept is the foundation of the OOA approach.

1.3.3 Information Modeling

Information modeling has evolved over a number of years. The primary modeling tool of information modeling—the entity-relationship diagram—has evolved into semantic data models. Modeling the world in data has helped capture problem space content.

Here's an equation to help identify this method:

Information Modeling =
    Objects
    + Attributes
    + Relationships
    + Supertype/Sub-types
    + Associative Objects.

The older strategy says: Develop an indented list of attributes. Put the attributes into object buckets. Add relationships. Refine with supertype/sub-types and associative objects. Then normalize.

The newer strategy is much the same, except that the initial step is to find objects in the real world, and describe them with attributes. Otherwise, one proceeds in basically the same fashion.

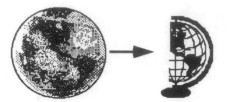

Figure 1.3: *Information Modeling Decomposition*

With the newer strategy, information modeling maps directly from the problem space to Objects in the model. This improvement in mapping is large, but a more detailed mapping is needed.

Information modeling is a partial method. It is well presented in several books (e.g., [Shlaer and Mellor, 1988]) and papers (e.g., [Loomis, Shaw, Rumbaugh, 1987]). Below is a list of missing concepts:

1. *Services:* the processing requirements for each Object, encapsulated and treated with the Attributes as an intrinsic whole.

2. *Inheritance:* explicit representation of Attribute and Service commonality.

3. *Messages:* a narrow, well-defined interface between Objects.

4. *Structure:* Classification Structure and Assembly Structure, as fundamental human methods of organization, are not central issues (but should be).

1.3.4 An Observation on Stability vs. Volatility

At issue is the impact of additions, extensions, changes, and deletions of features in the description of system requirements. This is especially important when considering "families" of systems—i.e., situations where a variety of implementations may be needed. Stability is also important throughout the *development* phase of a project, when over-optimistic goals need to be toned down from a full implementation (with adequate time, money, and people) to a lesser system—a phenomenon sometimes called "downsizing requirements."

Eventually one must address processes and sub-processes (functions/sub-functions). For example, Services will be needed to set up an instance of an Object, connect the instance to instances of other Objects, and provide on-going monitoring. Yet how much the players (customer, management, and technical staff) decide to automate this time and how sophisticated the Services may be are both quite volatile; they are continually subject to the triple constraint of capability, schedule, and budget.

External interfaces are the next most likely components to change. How smart or dumb are the devices? What do other systems need from the system under consideration? What does this system need from others? What requests will the human make as he uses the system?

The next part likely to change includes the data Attributes that describe items in the problem space. Yet these changes tend to apply to a single Object, e.g., the "Aircraft" Object and its Attributes, such as call number, serial number, location (latitude, longitude, altitude), and status.

The most stable aspects of a system, those which are least susceptible to potential change, are the Objects in the problem space. For example, whether one specifies a very low budget or a very sophisticated air traffic control system, one will still have the same basic Objects with which to organize the analysis and ultimately the specification: "Aircraft," "Controller," "Airspace," and the like. A more expensive system will have more Attributes for each Object. Also, a more expensive version will have more elaborate interfaces for monitoring devices and other systems (and additional Objects to model this). The more expensive system will have more sophisticated Services defined for each Object (e.g., "Aircraft" with an automated tracking Service, "Aircraft.Track"). Also, the more expensive version may have some additional Objects (e.g., a "Radar" Object, with corresponding Attributes, plus Services such as "Radar.Interrogate"). Yet by and large, the very stable aspect of the system (Objects in the problem space) will remain the same across what potentially could be major changes in scope of a software requirements activity.[5]

So in terms of approach, it's not that an analyst does not specify Services; this designation must be done, regardless of the simplicity or complexity of the system. It's what comes first, what predominates. The key to understanding problem space lies in deciding what is the primary view and the overall organization, communicating that understanding, and ultimately specifying requirements. Underlying OOA is the idea of using information hiding to hide the more volatile elements; with OOA, analysts base the overall structure of their thinking and specification on the more stable elements.

Consequently, as an overall structure in planning a Registration and Title System, an analyst looks at owners, vehicles, purchases, titles, registrations, and clerks, and then progressively adds layers of requirements development (Structures, Attributes, Connections, Services).

1.3.5 Object-Oriented

"Object-Oriented" is a difficult subject, because the term "Object" has come from two very different areas of study:

1. From Information Modeling, meaning a representation of some real-world thing, and some number of instances of that thing.

2. From Object-Oriented Programming Languages, meaning a run-time instance of some processing and values, defined by a static description called a "class."

---

[5] Of course, *all* systems are susceptible to change, and OOA systems are just as susceptible as any other. But with OOA, the impact of the change is more easily identified, bounded, traced, and assessed.

It has been reported that some conference presentations have been overrun with lengthy discussions over what the word "Object" really means.

An equation for recognizing an object-oriented approach follows:

Object-Oriented =

Objects
   (an encapsulation of Attributes and exclusive Services; an abstraction of something in the problem space, with some number of instances in the problem space)
+ Classification
+ Inheritance
+ Communication with messages.

One can look at different languages, environments, methods, and books and ask "Are they really object-oriented?" Unfortunately, many times the answer is "no"; object-oriented suffers from being a catchy marketing phrase, used at times to mean "the good stuff."

Is Ada an object-oriented language? No. Genericity, that is, typed parameters, is convenient, but no substitute for inheritance. In fact, to provide the missing classification and inheritance, one software vendor (Software Productivity Solutions of Melbourne, Florida) markets a preprocessor to Ada.

Is Information Modeling object-oriented (e.g., *Object-Oriented Systems Analysis* [Shlaer and Mellor, Stephen, 1988], a book better titled "Making Semantic Data Modeling Practical")? No. Services are missing. Classification is missing. Inheritance is missing.

OOA builds upon the best concepts from Information Modeling (entity-relationship diagrams and semantic data models) and the best concepts from Object-Oriented Programming Languages.

From Information Modeling comes Attributes, Relationships, Structure, and the representation of an Object as some number of instances of something in the problem space. From Object-Oriented Programming Languages comes the encapsulation of Attributes and exclusive Services, the treatment of Attributes and Services as an intrinsic whole, the portrayal of Classification Structure, and the explicit expression of commonality via inheritance.

Instead of an indirect mapping from problem space to function/sub-function or problem space to flows and bubbles, the mapping is direct, from the problem space to the model: "Aircraft," "Radar," "Airspace," and "Controller" Objects; "Owner," "Vehicle," "Purchase," "Registration," "Title," and "Clerk" Objects.

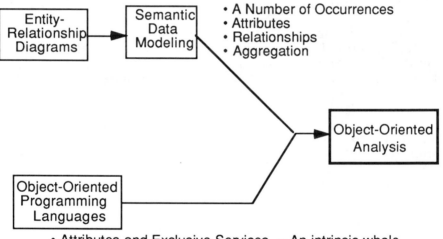

Figure 1.4: *The Formulation of OOA*

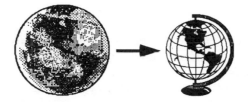

Figure 1.5: *Object-Oriented Decomposition*

OOA is based on the uniform application of:

- pervading methods of organization.
  ... the overall framework for both analysis and specification.

- communication with messages.
  ...the interaction between the user and system.
  ...the interaction between instances in the system.

- behavior classification.
  ...the overall framework for identifying services to be provided by each component.

The differences between the various analysis methods are summarized in the table below:

PRINCIPLES

METHODS	Abstraction Procedural	Data	Encapsulation	Classification & Inheritance	Methods of Organization	Behavior Categories
METHODS						
Functional Decomposition	x					
Data Flow Information Modeling (Data Only)	x			x	x	x
Object-Oriented	x	x	x	x	x	x

Why OOA? Seven prime reasons:

1. It defines and communicates requirements within the framework of the *three basic methods of human organization* (Object and Attributes, Classification Structure, and Assembly Structure).

2. It focuses primarily on *problem space understanding.*

3. It treats Attributes and exclusive Services on those Attributes as an *intrinsic whole.*

4. It analyzes and specifies using *self-contained* partitioning (minimal dependency between one Object and others).

5. It gains leverage through *explicit representation of commonality.*

6. It applies a *consistent, powerful underlying representation* for Analysis (what is to be built) and Design (how it is to be built this time).

7. It accommodates *families* of systems, and accommodates ongoing practical tradeoffs.

In an overall approach, OOA consists of five major steps:

> Identifying Objects
> Identifying Structures
> Defining Subjects
> Defining Attributes (and Instance Connections)
> Defining Services (and Message Connections).

The acronym OSSAS serves as a convenient reminder of the first five steps.

Once the model is built, it is presented and reviewed in five major layers:

Subject layer
Object layer
Structure layer
Attribute layer
Service layer.

An example of these five layers follows.

Figure 1.6: *An OOA Example: Subject Layer*

Subject layer. A Subject is a mechanism for controlling how much of a model that a reader considers at one time.

This model consists of four Subjects (refer to Figure 1.6). The level of abstraction is based upon the Structures and Connections in subsequent layers.

Object layer. An Object is an abstraction of data and exclusive processing on that data, reflecting the capabilities of a system to keep information about or interact with something in the real world.

The example consists of six Objects—an external system ("Vehicle"), an event remembered over time ("Title," "Registration"), roles played by humans ("Owner," "Clerk"), and an organizational unit ("Organization"). (Refer to Figure 1.7.)

Subject lines are included to guide the reader through sections of large models.

Structure layer. Structure represents complexity in a problem space. Classification Structure portrays class-member organization, reflecting generalization-specialization.

Assembly Structure shows aggregation, reflecting whole and component parts.

Structure reflects problem space complexity, capitalizing on two of the pervading methods of organization used by humans. In addition, Classification Structure provides a basis for subsequent inheritance, giving explicit representation of Attribute and Service commonality within such a structure. However, note that abstraction in OOA is accomplished primarily with Objects and Subjects; only in a secondary way is abstraction accomplished with the levels in a Classification Structure.

The model includes two Classification Structures (Legal and Vehicle) (refer to Figure 1.8). It also includes one Assembly Structure (an Organization and its clerks).

Attribute layer. An Attribute is a data element used to describe an instance of an Object or Classification Structure. Attributes are shown on the diagram and specified in the Object Repository. (The Repository consists of the five OOA layers and supporting template-based documentation.)

Attributes are listed in the center section of the Object and Structure symbols. Attributes are data elements or logical groupings of data elements. (Refer to Figure 1.9.)

Note that the Attributes pertaining to all vehicles are defined higher in the Classification Structure, and are extended by the specializations (Car, Truck, and Motorcycle) lower in the Structure.

Instance Connections represent a mapping of an instance of an Object or Classification Structure with other instance(s); they are shown with a solid line, with markings indicating multiplicity and participation constraints.

Service layer. A Service is the processing to be performed upon receipt of a message. Services are identified on the diagram and specified in the Object Repository.

Services are listed in the bottom section of the Object and Structure symbols. Services to add, change, delete, and select a Service are implicit to each Object and Structure (and so do not appear in the diagram, although such Services are defined in the Object Repository). The Object Services show the processing encapsulated with the Attributes (refer to Figure 1.10). Certain Services (e.g., add, change, delete) are implicit, and are generally not shown on the diagram; other Services (e.g., CalculateFee) are explicitly shown.

The primary strategy focuses on three fundamental Services: "Occur" (add, change, delete, test, select, and connect an occurrence), "Calculate," and "Monitor." Secondary strategies examine state-event-response (causation) and Object life history.

Note that Services pertaining to all vehicles are defined higher in the Classification Structure, and are extended by the specializations (Car, Truck, and Motorcycle) lower in the structure.

Message Connections represent the sending of a message from one Object to another, to get some processing done on their behalf. They are shown with dashed arrows, pointing from the sender of the message to the receiver of the message.

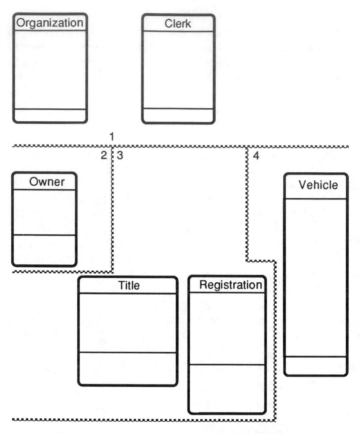

Figure 1.7: *An OOA Example: Object Layer*

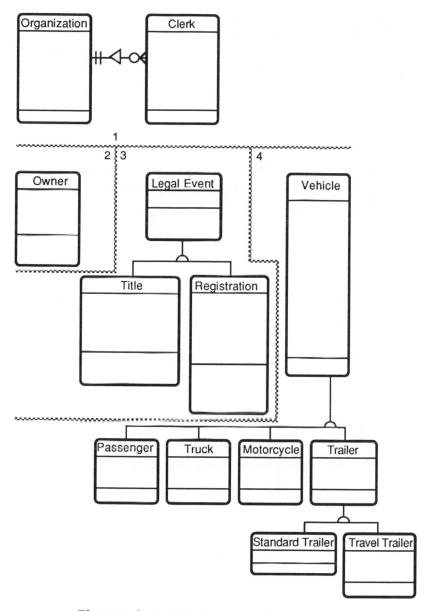

Figure 1.8: *An OOA Example: Structure Layer*

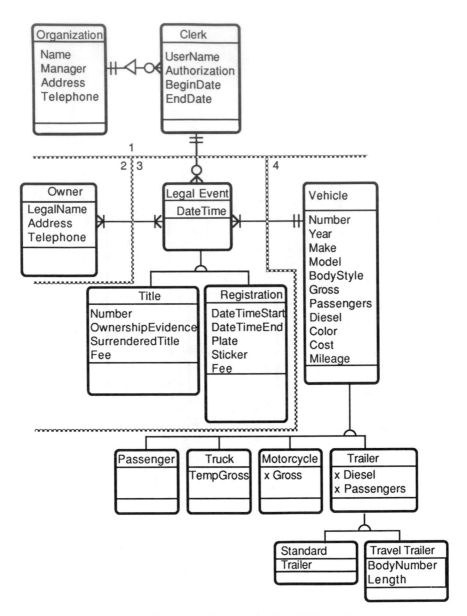

Figure 1.9: *An OOA Example: Attribute Layer*

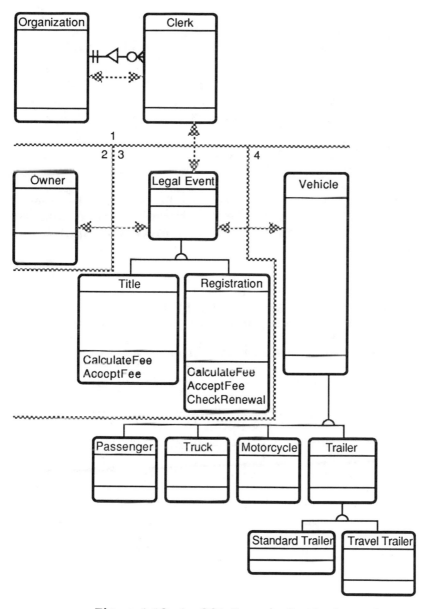

Figure 1.10: *An OOA Example: Service Layer*

2 EXPERIENCING AN OBJECT PERSPECTIVE

This chapter addresses some very specific concepts of object-orientedness. To drive the concepts home experientially, we use the language Smalltalk as a convenient vehicle of communication. This usage does not suggest that Smalltalk itself is an OOA tool or that one *must* use an object-oriented programming language in order to practice OOA (although prototypes and demonstration programs used to better understand requirements could be built from OOA models using Smalltalk). Rather, the chapter uses Smalltalk, a full object-oriented language and environment, to elucidate certain critical aspects that are object-oriented.

In 1987, the U.S. Naval Weapons Center asked one of the authors to conduct a one-week workshop on Object-Oriented Software Engineering. They wanted to explore what was so important about this approach; in effect, they asked: *what's the big deal about object-oriented anything?*

So we began to investigate the underlying object-oriented principles that could be applied to programming languages, then to design, then back to analysis. We spent the first three days immersing ourselves in a fully object-oriented language and environment: Smalltalk. We executed many, many Smalltalk examples. *Everything* in Smalltalk is object-oriented, so one gets fully immersed in an object-oriented perspective.

Similarly, we recommend that you, the reader, take the time to explore Smalltalk. We recommend the Smalltalk products from Digitalk for the IBM PC and Macintosh because they're reasonably priced and come with over 200 ready-to-run examples; for the Mac, consider Smalltalk from Parc Place Systems.[1] By working through a series of graduated examples, you can work first-hand with a fully object-oriented language and environment. The experience is worthwhile, even for those who no longer write programs for a living.

The end of this chapter focuses on the key points for us as requirements analysts, preparing to apply OOA in day-to-day work.

2.1 SMALLTALK

Welcome to Smalltalk, a fully object-oriented language and environment.

In Smalltalk, everything is based on Objects. For example, integers are Objects, panes are Objects, and even the language syntax itself consists of Objects. And together with Objects is the notion of sending Messages to Objects to get things done.

This fully object-oriented arena captures a fundamentally different perspective than the one most programmers are familiar with. The following sections will delve into it with examples of Smalltalk Objects, Methods, Messages, Classes, and Inheritance.

2.2 SMALLTALK OBJECTS

A Smalltalk Object is an encapsulation of information and the description of its manipulation. It has a private data structure and corresponding Methods (services, processing) that can be performed on that data structure. In other words, an Object has data inside, and knows what to do with that data.

---

[1] This is not intended as an endorsement of the IBM PC or the Macintosh, nor either version of Smalltalk. Indeed, both versions of Smalltalk are available on a number of additional hardware platforms.

4

Figure 2.1: *An Integer Object*

This figure is a representation of an integer Object, with the value 4. The data structure and Methods appropriate for the data structure (integer) are treated as an intrinsic whole. And the interface is kept very narrow—the only way to manipulate the data structure is by using visible Methods.

'this is fun'

Figure 2.2: *A String Object*

This Object is a string Object. It not only has the data structure "this is fun" hidden inside of it, but also it knows what actions are appropriate for the data structure. The Object knows, for example, that it is meaningless to compute the square root of "this is fun," but it is meaningful to compute the length of the string and return the result as an integer.

#(7 6 5 4 3)

Figure 2.3: *An Array of Objects*

This Object is actually an array of Objects (here the Objects in the array happen to all be integer Objects). And the Object shown in Figure 2.3 knows what to do with its internal data structure, and what actions are pertinent to arrays of Objects.

a Pane

Figure 2.4: *A Pane Object*

This Object is more sophisticated. It's an Object that corresponds to a window on a display device. It hides a data structure inside, and knows the actions that are appropriate for panes.

2.3 SMALLTALK MESSAGES

A Smalltalk Message tells an Object what to do.

> A Message says:
>> Here's the Object that gets the Message
>>> (called the "receiver Object").
>> Here's the Method I want done now
>>> (called the "Method selector").
>> Here are the arguments to use.

The operation is named in the Message, but what is done is actually hidden (encapsulated) in the Object that receives the Message.

A Smalltalk Message is a selection of one of the manipulations that an Object knows how to perform. A Message says "do this one," and the Object itself knows what actions to carry out in response.

This perspective is fundamentally different from the *procedural* perspective almost all software engineers learned in their introductory programming courses. When first using Smalltalk, many users try to map Messages into a familiar function or procedure-call format. But the mapping is hard to maintain. So after a while, one begins to think of Objects as strong encapsulations of data and processing on that data; when a Message is indeed sent to the Object, the Object does its thing, and then a response is received from the Object.

Some examples follow:

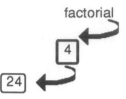

Figure 2.5: *The Factorial Example*

In this example, the Message "factorial" is sent to an integer Object. Hidden inside the Object is its current value, 4. The Message tells the Object what to do. The Object has a corresponding Method describing what it is to do upon receipt of the Message. Notice the strong encapsulation of data and the processing on that data. The Object with the value 4 does its work, and then returns the result (which is itself an object)—an integer Object with the value 24. So what it means to "compute factorial" is hidden inside the Object; the interface between the Object and other Objects is specified with visible Methods; and the means for getting things done is sending Messages to invoke services.

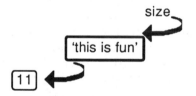

Figure 2.6: *The Size Example*

In this example, the Message "size" is being sent to a string Object. The Object knows what to do upon receipt of such a Message, and it sends back a result (which happens to be an integer Object).

Figure 2.7: *An Example with an Array Object*

This third example involves an Object with a little more sophistication—it's an array Object. It understands Messages pertinent to its data structure. The Message sent to the Object is "at: 2" (read as "at colon two"), which is a Method selector and one argument. The Object does its work, and returns an integer Object with the value 6 as the result.

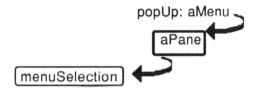

Figure 2.8: *A Pane Object*

The fourth example hides even more elaborate data and processing on that data. The Message "popUp: aMenu" is sent; meaning "here's the Service (popUp) and here's the argument you'll need (aMenu)." The Object does all of the work of putting up the pop-up menu, getting a valid selection, removing the pop-up menu, and returning an object containing the menu selection.

2.4 SMALLTALK CLASSES

In addition to Objects and Messages, Smalltalk has Classes. All object-oriented programming languages have such mechanisms. In Smalltalk, it's a mechanism for *classifying* data structures and processing according to their similarities and special-case extensions.

Smalltalk Classes express static descriptions of data and Methods. Objects are run-time instances of a Class. For example, the "Integer" Class defines the hidden data structure and the Methods that apply to integers. At run time, a programmer can create an instance of a Class, give it a value (via a Message) and start doing things with it (again via Messages).

It's classification itself that's of interest here. Generalization/specialization help us capture problem space structure by explicitly representing commonality using *inheritance*. Analysts are not particularly interested in the static vs. run-time distinctions imposed by this particular programming language; such a notion does not have a place in OOA. But the concepts of classification (generalization/specialization) and inheritance are very powerful ideas and are very useful in analysis.

Consider two Smalltalk Class examples.

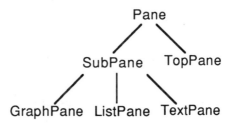

Figure 2.9: *An Example of Generalization/Specialization*

A pane is a window sub-area in a display device. Pane can be specialized into a SubPane (which knows about scroll bars) and a TopPane (which is responsible for an entire window). A SubPane is further specialized (extended) into a GraphPane (with data structure and Methods for graphics), ListPane (with data structures and Methods for list manipulation and item selection), and TextPane (with data structures and Methods for text editing). Observe that the Classes organize the definition of Attributes and Services according to their similarities at a higher level, and then extends or specializes those Attributes and Services at lower levels.

Collection	contain a number of objects
Bag	collection of unordered elements in which duplicates are allowed
Indexed Collection	collection with index
Fixed Size Collection	fixed indexable sequence
Array	fixed indexable sequence of objects
ByteArray	fixed indexable sequence of bytes
String	fixed indexable sequence of characters
Symbol	unique fixed size sequence of characters
Ordered Collection	collection which can grow
Sorted Collection	collection sorted by instantiated compare code
Set	unordered collection of unique objects
Dictionary	collection of unique key & value pairs
SymbolSet	collection of unique fixed size sequences of chars

Figure 2.10: *Another Example of Generalization/Specialization*

The second example of Smalltalk Classes also illustrates the theme of generalization/specialization, this time with some lower level data structures and Methods. Remember that everything in Smalltalk is set up with Classes—it's where the data structures and Methods are defined. So again observe this hierarchical patterning of general to specific, or of basic capability and extension of that capability.

For an object-oriented programming language, tools are needed to browse a Class hierarchy—it may end up being 5 or more levels deep, and may consist of 200 or more classes. With such depth of Classes, browsing tools are needed so that the "ripple effect" of a change at a higher level can be controlled on lower levels.[2] Usually this type of control means displaying a Class on the screen, along with its inherited data structures and Methods; this area is one of continued research. However, such tools are not needed for OOA; from our consulting experience, we found that Classification Structures were usually expressed with only two levels, and did not exceed four levels.

---

[2] Note that we usually don't need browsers for OOA models. The number of classes in the OOA modeling domain is much less than the number of classes one might use in an object-oriented programming language like Smalltalk.

2.5 SMALLTALK INHERITANCE

Hand-in-hand with Smalltalk Classes comes Smalltalk Inheritance.

Inheritance is a mechanism that simplifies the definition of software components that are similar to those previously defined.

The benefit of inheritance in an object-oriented programming language is that a designer/implementer can say, "Yes, I want to reuse what you've got there, except that I want to add these data structures, and add to or extend the processing in this fashion. It's just like this, but a little bit different." This attitude is vastly different than, and worlds apart from, saying "OK. So this is what you built. And I've got to use it as-is, or else go off and write my own."

Inheritance is a powerful mechanism for reuse, and for explicitly capturing commonality. It consists of four major aspects:

1. For each Class, the Class shares the data structure defined in its Superclasses (those Classes above it, working up through the hierarchy).

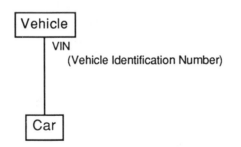

Figure 2.11: *Sharing Superclass Data Structures*

(e.g., Vehicle Identification Number (VIN) is defined for Vehicle, and inherited by Car.)

2. For each Class, the Class shares the Methods defined in its Superclasses.

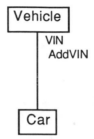

Figure 2.12: *Sharing Superclass Methods*

(e.g., AddVIN is defined for Vehicle, and inherited by Car.)

3. For each Class, the Class can add to the data structure.

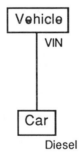

Figure 2.13: *Adding to an Existing Data Structure*

(e.g., Diesel is defined as applicable to a Car, but not to all vehicles.)

4. For each Class, the Class can add to or extend (or in the case of Smalltalk, even override) inherited Methods.

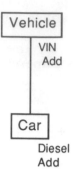

Figure 2.14: *Adding to Inherited Methods*

(e.g., Add is defined for Vehicle, and then extended for Car.)

Thus, the bottom-line benefit of inheritance is that it gives us a basis for explicitly capturing commonality of Attributes and exclusive Services on those Attributes.

Here are some inheritance examples from Smalltalk:

```
Pane              menu, pop-up, font—for a window sub-area
    SubPane       scroll bar
      GraphPane   bitmap
                  basic graphics tool (points, corners)
      ListPane    indexed collection of strings
      TextPane    strings
                  display, scroll, edit (append, search & replace)
      TopPane     color, border, frame, label
                  (a pane responsible for an entire window)
```

Figure 2.15: *A Smalltalk Inheritance Example*

Panes know about data structures and Methods pertinent to a window sub-area, and the corresponding menus, pop-ups, and fonts; SubPanes add capability, with knowledge of the data structures and Methods pertinent to scroll bars hidden inside; GraphPanes carry the data structure and Methods even further, with a hidden bitmap and graphic tools; and so on.

Note the generalization (commonality) at the higher levels, followed by the extension in special cases in lower levels, all expressed succinctly with inheritance. Effectively, you see an adding on of data structures and processing sophistication as you work your way down the hierarchy.

Collection	add,...
Bag	add, ...
Indexed Collection	...
Fixed Size Collection	add,...
Array	...
ByteArray	...
String	edit,...
Symbol	...
Ordered Collection	add,...
Sorted Collection	add,...
Set	...
Dictionary	add,...
SymbolSet	add,...

Figure 2.16: *Another Inheritance Example*

The second example illustrates how one Method, "Add," gets extended again and again as one moves down the hierarchy. New Methods can be added at whatever level is appropriate, e.g., the "Edit" Method shown in the example.

2.6 KEY POINTS

So what are the key lessons to be extracted from this small taste of Smalltalk?

1. Attributes and exclusive Services on the Attributes are treated as an intrinsic whole.

2. The interface between Objects is fully defined by the Services (Methods) that are visible to other Objects. The only way one can get to the data hidden inside an Object is by sending a Message to an Object, corresponding to a Service provided by that Object.

3.   Classification Structure and Inheritance provide ways to model problem space generalization/specialization, and then gain leverage by explicitly expressing commonality of data and processing at the upper levels, and then extending the data and processing at lower levels.

INTRODUCTION TO CHAPTERS 3-7

The chapters that follow cover the five major steps of OOA.

Each step is structured into four sections:
What
Why
How to Define
Key Points.

The "Key Points" sections summarize the step, with
Notation
Crib Sheet
    (concise definitions and strategy)
Example—Sensor System
Example—Registration and Title System
Example—Real-Time Airlift System.

TERMINOLOGY MAP

At this introductory stage, we feel it would be helpful to introduce a "terminology map," specifically for those readers already familiar with object-oriented programming languages or semantic data modeling.   Our rationale is to select a consistent set of terms that are descriptive in the context of analysis and specification, but which do not imply a particular implementation technology (e.g., the choice of a programming language).

Semantic Data modeling	OOPL	OOA
Object	Class	Object
Attribute	Variable	Attribute
---	Method	Service
Occurrence	Instance	Instance
Supertype/subtype	Superclass/subclass	Classification Structure
Aggregation	---	Assembly Structure
Relationship	---	Instance Connection
---	Message	Message Connection

Some additional notes on terminology include:

1. Semantic data modeling pertains only to data, not to the processing on that data.

2. In much of the object-oriented literature, "Classification Structure" is referred to as "Objects and Sub-objects." "Assembly Structure" is referred to as "nested sub-objects."

3. Objects are often referred to as actors, servers, and agents. Actors send Messages to other Objects; senders receive Messages from other Objects; and agents do both. OOA Objects exhibit such behavior; OOA simply does not introduce these additional terms.

4. Some OOPLs make a distinction between subclassing versus subtyping. Subclassing allows

unrestricted inheritance. Subtyping provides for a stricter inheritance: an instance of a subtype can always be used in place of a supertype.

3 IDENTIFYING OBJECTS

The objects are just there for the picking.
[Meyer, 1988]

Nuts! Even back in the days of Entity-Relationship methodologies, identifying Objects was never intuitively obvious. And, even with a data-oriented perspective, the systems analyst must eventually specify the functionality of the system. (We will do so, in the context of each Object, in the "Defining Services" step discussed in Chapter 7.)

This chapter presents specific guidelines for identifying Objects. We begin by defining what we mean by "object," and then describe why objects play such an important role in the specification of a system. The meat of the chapter includes *where to look* for Objects; *what to look for*; *what to consider*; *what to challenge*; and *how to name* Objects.

3.1 OBJECTS—WHAT

The general definition of an object is:

> An object is a package of information and a description of its manipulation. [Oxford, 1986]

The OOA-specific definition is:

> An Object is an encapsulation and an abstraction: an encapsulation of Attributes and exclusive Services on those Attributes; an abstraction of the problem space, representing one or more occurrences of something in the problem space.

57

The encapsulation of Attributes and exclusive Services on those Attributes has great impact on the stability of the OOA model. First, this encapsulation forms the basis for treating the Attributes and corresponding Services as an intrinsic whole. Analysts focus on a system's stored data and processing *together*. Separating process analysis from data analysis is not even a consideration—both must be considered as an intrinsic whole, Object by Object. Second, encapsulation helps reduce subsequent re-work, structuring the overall analysis and specification strategy upon a framework that is likely to be much more stable over time:

Interfaces between system components—highly volatile
Functions—very volatile
Sequencing of functions—very volatile
Data, held over time—less volatile
Problem Space Objects—the least volatile.

The activity of abstracting one or more occurrences of a "thing" in the problem space also has impact. Analysts first must understand the problem domain at hand; it makes little sense to run off and start writing air traffic control functional requirements, without first studying, expressing, and validating our understanding of what air traffic control is really all about. Defining Objects as an abstraction of the real world helps us gain significant problem space understanding—which we document in the form of a *system model*. Ultimately this system model results in a tangible, reviewable, and manageable collection of model layers (Subject, Object, Structure, Attribute, Connection, and Service) produced during the five major steps of OOA.

The system model also provides a basis for an initial expression of the system *context*. Context is not defined by a diagram, drawn by a systems analyst making a technical decision. In contrast, customers, managers, analysts, competitors, government regulators, and standards bearers all affect the system context over time. System context is an indication of how much of the problem space will be embraced by the automated system, what data will be held over time, how much processing sophistication will be included—all within the "quadruple constraint" inspired by [Rosenau, 1981] that affects all systems:

Quadruple Constraint =   Budget
                         + Schedule
                         + Capability
                         + People.

System context is set by quadruple constraint negotiations.   To control a project, a manager must be accountable in all four areas (perhaps you've known highly acclaimed managers who were always fine on budget and schedule, but were never held accountable for the content (capability) of their delivered results).   All four constraints must be respected.

Objects represent the initial expression of context. And the subsequent OOA steps provide an increasingly detailed description of the context in terms of Structures, Connections, Attributes, and ultimately Services (processing capability—how sophisticated the system will be this time).

3.2   OBJECTS—WHY

The primary motivation for identifying Objects is to match the technical representation of a system more closely to the conceptual view of the real world. As noted earlier, analysis notation and strategy are based upon three basic human methods of organization: Objects and Attributes, Classification (classes and members), and Assembly (whole and parts).

Another motivation for emphasizing Objects is our desire to create a stable framework for examining the problem space and then levying requirements. The Objects in an air traffic control system today will probably be the same as the Objects in an air traffic control system five years from now— but the functions and procedures for manipulating those Objects may have changed radically. Objects are relatively stable.

A final motivation is to avoid shifting the underlying representation as we move from systems analysis to design. The gap, or "twilight zone," between analysis and design seemed impenetrable throughout the 1970s and 1980s: people have pondered the subject, drawn cartoons, and presented papers at seminars and conferences. Yet shifting from an underlying network organization for analysis (data flow diagrams) to an underlying hierarchical organization for design (structure charts) has been too magical for most practitioners and nearly always untraceable (a key issue of concern on large, critical systems such as those developed for the U.S. Department of Defense). And, recent attempts to transform an underlying network organization for analysis (data flow diagrams) to an underlying Object representation (Object-Oriented Design (OOD)) have met the same problem. The heart of design is taking the requirements and adding implementation detail to them—and that job is challenging enough. Throwing in a change in underlying representation has been the root of the analysis/design chasm. We can end this dilemma by using an object-oriented representation in analysis, design, and implementation (using an object-oriented programming language is not required in applying OOA or OOD, but helpful during implementation).

3.3 OBJECTS—HOW TO DEFINE

The steps in "How to Define" have come from practice and experience in the field, based upon Objects found initially, as well as ones found later (and investigating why they were missed earlier).

3.3.1 Where to Look

Look at problem space, text, and pictures.

First, look at the problem space. Study the problem domain itself—the world of the user. This examination involves some investigative research. The user can typically supply some form of system requirements, from a several-sentence description up to several-ream descriptions. But before diving into the details, first invest some time learning about the problem domain.

Ask the user for a concise summary of, say, 25, 50, or even 100 pages about the subject matter. Go to Encyclopedia Britannica's Macropaedia for a 10-12 page professionally-written description of the problem space under consideration; this is an excellent way to learn the terminology and fundamentals of a topic—e.g., air traffic control. Such investigative research pays off handsomely in rapidly gaining a broader perspective of the problem space at hand.

It's also helpful to spend time sitting with and listening to the people for whom the automated capability will be provided; that a consumer of services and his needs are worthy of careful consideration—e.g., the pressures associated with being an air traffic controller.

Follow through with additional reading. Scan whatever you can get your hands on, and set aside those sections that especially illuminate the subject matter and deserve detailed study and consideration. As you read, consider the nouns in the written material; these words will often give you a clue about potential Objects in the system. This doesn't mean that you should simply circle the nouns and declare them Objects (as some writers have proposed). Real systems are not that simple to analyze; more guidelines are needed. Read extensively, consider the nouns, and weigh them against the criteria presented below in "What to Consider" and "What to Challenge."

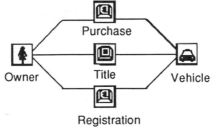

Figure 3.1: *Picture Showing Potential Objects*

Follow through with pictures. Collect any pictures you can—block diagrams, interface diagrams, system component diagrams, very high level data and/or control flow diagrams.[1] In addition, draw plenty of your own pictures, using icons and lines between them as initial sketches of the problem space, and how the pieces interact with each other.

Hence, look at problem space, text, and pictures.

3.3.2   What to Look For

To find potential Objects, look for: structure, other systems, devices, events remembered, roles played, locations, and organizational units. The items discussed here are presented in the order of most fruitful Object finders first.

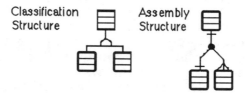

Figure 3.2: *Structure*

Structure. Structure is so significant for finding Objects and representing problem space hierarchy that it has its own step in the OOA method (*Identifying Structure*, the next step in the OOA method, is discussed in Chapter 4). Classification Structures and Assembly Structures are most fruitful; they bring strong intellectual leverage to the table. We will discuss both forms of structure in detail in Chapter 4.

---

[1] Note that this means you will be looking at prior mappings of the problem space to an automated system. This is often a good way to check for potentially missing objects and attributes that may be needed in the new system.

Figure 3.3: *Other Systems*

Other Systems.   What other systems and "external terminators" will the system under consideration interact with?   This interaction could be hard-wired (e.g., a cable between systems), transmission interaction (e.g., an aircraft automatically reporting its altitude), or instance interaction (e.g., a vehicle in a registration and title system).

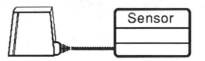

Figure 3.4: *Devices*

Devices.   What devices will the system under study need to interact with?   Some devices may exchange data and control information with the system.   Do not add implementation-specific computer components (c.g., disk drives and display terminals); defer such considerations, keeping notes in a folder until the design phase of the project. You'll keep the requirements simpler this way, and avoid major re-work when the "unchangeable" computer components suddenly change on you.

Figure 3.5: *Events Remembered*

Events remembered. Next, consider the problem space for an event remembered. Is there a point in time or an historical event that must be observed and recorded by the system? For example, the point in time in which someone gets a title for a motor vehicle must be remembered; it's a legal event, and certain data must be captured by statute, e.g., the type of ownership evidence presented. On the other hand, if a system monitors a nuclear reactor, and an incident occurs, then information must be kept about that historical event, over time: who, what, when, where, how, why.

Figure 3.6: *Roles Played*

Roles Played. What roles do human beings play with the system under study? Objects representing people pop up in two ways: those representing a user of the system (e.g., a clerk who interacts with the system), and those representing people who do not interact directly with the system, but about whom information is kept by the system (e.g., motor vehicle owner). Owners and clerks are both reasonably human, yet they play different roles in the system; subsequent investigation of Attributes and Services will capture the distinction in detail.

Figure 3.7: *Locations*

Locations. What physical locations, offices, or sites does the system under consideration need knowledge of? For example, consider an embedded system that will be set up and configured at a particular latitude, longitude, altitude, and terrain profile. A site object may keep track of the Attributes of one or many sites; it depends upon the problem space under consideration.

Figure 3.8: *Organizational Units*

Organizational Units. What organizational units do the humans belong to? For example, a motor vehicle clerk works within a county organization—so "County" should be considered as a potential Object. And, if the system needs to keep track of information about a county (e.g., manager name, address, fee percentages, and the like) or provide processing pertinent to a county (e.g., determine how much money was collected today), then the Object is needed.

So as an analyst, look for structure, other systems, devices, events remembered, roles played, locations, and organizational units. Once you find a candidate Object, examine it in light of "What to Consider" and "What to Challenge."

3.3.3   What to Consider

You've found a candidate Object. Perhaps you found another called "Vehicle." Should you include it as an Object in your model?

Consider:

•   needed remembrance

•   needed Services

•   more than one Attribute

- common Attributes

- common Services

- essential requirements.

Think about these things when determining whether or not to include the Object in the model.

Figure 3.9: *Needed Remembrance*

Needed remembrance. Does the system need to remember anything about this Object? Look at the problem space. Can an occurrence of the Object be described? What are some of the potential Attributes? For example, potential Attributes for a clerk include name, password, and authorization. Is knowledge about that real world thing of interest to the system under consideration? Is there something about an occurrence of the Object that the system needs to remember? If not, the validity and relevance of the Object is suspect—remember, many Objects in the real world may be interesting, and may come up in discussions with the users, but they may not turn out to be relevant to the system.

Figure 3.10: *Needed Services*

Needed Services. Does the system need to provide processing on behalf of this Object? As long as needed remembrance applies, then Services will be needed—at the very least to maintain occurrences of the Object. No problem: we probably have a valid Object.

However, an Object may have required Services, but no required remembrance (Attributes). For example, we might identify a "User" Object in a problem space where the system does not need to keep any information about the user. In this case, the system does not need the usual identification number, name, access privileges, and the like. However, the system does need to monitor the user, responding to requests and providing timely information. And so, because of required Services on behalf of the real world thing (in this case, User), we need to add a corresponding Object to the model of the problem space.

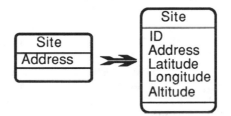

Figure 3.11: *More than One Attribute*

More than one Attribute. This criterion helps filter out potential Objects when an analyst gets to a level that is too low in his thinking. If an Object (e.g., "Location") has one Attribute (e.g., also "Location"), get suspicious; it's likely that "Location" may be better included as an Attribute, which may appear in a number of Objects, rather than as an individual Object in its own right. The key is the leveling of detail: Objects are further described by Attributes, which are then further described in an Attribute Dictionary.

Figure 3.12: *Common Attributes*

Common Attributes. Can you identify a set of Attributes that apply to every single occurrence of an Object? Every time a system knows about the occurrence of an Object, it should have a value for each Attribute. For example, a "Home" Object in a real estate listing system might include location, price, "listed since" date, size, number of bedrooms, and number of bathrooms—each Attribute would apply to each occurrence of the "Home" Object. However, if at times only certain Attributes apply (e.g., the Attribute "Diesel" applies only to certain types of motor vehicles, and is not applicable to others), it's an indication that a Classification Structure exists; we'll discuss this subject in more detail in Chapter 4.

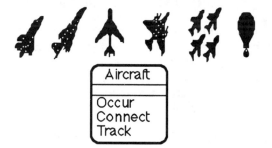

Figure 3.13: *Common Services*

Common Services. Can you identify a common set of Services—i.e., processing that applies to each occurrence of an Object? Processing may be needed to create an occurrence of an Object, establish connections between Objects, and provide on-going monitoring of occurrences of an Object. If the Services are the same for each occurrence, that's fine; however, if the Services vary depending on the type of occurrence, that variation is an indication that a Classification Structure exists.

This discussion indicates that you should consider common Attributes and Services in a general sense while investigating the problem space for an initial set of Objects. Then, as you consider the Attributes and Services in greater detail, you'll discover finer detail and nuances that you can bring into the model as well.

Essential requirements. Essential requirements are those requirements the system *must* have, regardless of the computer technology used to build (design and implement) the system. When radars and sensors (e.g., devices that measure temperature, pressure, or power) are in the problem space, then regardless of the computer technology that will eventually be employed, we should expect to see corresponding "Radar" and "Sensor" Objects. But system architectures (centralized, distributed, or replicated), disk drives, display terminals, batching up of computational results for better (faster) processing, time vs. size trade-offs, and the like are design and implementation considerations. Whether a design team chooses one or two computers is a design issue; so is the packing and shipping, and receiving and routing of requests and updates between machines. Whether the project chooses to use a hand held display device, a lap-top, a sophisticated graphics system, or large screen display is a design selection; as an analyst, focus on determining what information is required by the human using the system. Use prototypes and operational concept studies to define and refine what required information content is all about. But particular screen sequences, menus, windows and the like belong in a design folder, and ultimately in the design; they are mechanisms for implementing the requirements specified as to what the system must produce for its user.

Keep a file of design notes. It helps keep frustration down. And it helps people avoid premature design decisions or biases. Several months later, a design idea may or may not appear quite so appealing. And either way, the systems analysis and specification are not burdened with particular implementation details. They remain focused as abstractions, emphasizing the problem space and its Objects, Structures, Attributes, Connections, and Services.

It is fair game for an analyst to impose design constraints. For example, if a particular algorithm *must* be used—e.g., because of some legal statute—make it a requirement. Otherwise, specify the accuracy of the determined value, and allow the designer to select the algorithm appropriate in the context of the available computing resources.

The design team will add Objects to provide design-dependent processing—e.g., Objects to handle interfaces to other systems (pack and ship requests and data; receive and route requests and data), and Objects to handle a particular display technology (perhaps with windows and a limited amount of related information portrayed in each window, avoiding cognitive overload). So, check on Objects to be certain you are not moving ahead with particular implementation technology or interim batching decisions.

Even if a particular hardware/software architecture is mandated by the customer or by some external statute, and will never, ever change, keep it out of the systems analysis, organization, and specification. Why? First, to keep the analysis and specification abstractions as simple as possible. Second, to avoid massive rework when the never-ever-changeable does indeed change.

In conclusion, consider needed remembrance, needed Services, more than one Attribute, common Attributes, common Services, and essential requirements.

3.3.4   What to Challenge

Challenge:

- unneeded remembrance
- unneeded Services

- single occurrences
- derived results.

If a system does not need to hold information about a real world thing over time or provide Services for it, remove the Object. This situation frequently occurs during discussions with a customer, reviewing the initial model (the Object layer). So, this issue becomes a "scope" issue, with the triple constraint of time, schedule, and capability. As an analyst, push the edges of the problem space at hand, to consider implicit or forgotten requirements; it may be critical to a system's usefulness. A mental approach to looking at the edges is to seek out neighboring problem "sub-spaces," to examine Objects (and Structures) that lie just beyond the system requested by the customer.

Next, challenge single occurrence Objects (for those Objects that have Attributes, and are not just Service-only Objects). If an Object with a single occurrence really does reflect the problem space, so be it. For example, an air traffic control system might have

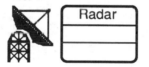

Figure 3.14: *A Single-Occurrence Object*

a "Radar" Object, with only one radar in the problem space. Or there might be a "Commander-In-Chief" Object at the root of an Assembly Structure. But if another Object with the same Attributes and same Services exists, and if it accurately reflects the reality of the problem domain, then consider using just one Object instead. And, if another Object with similar Attributes and similar Services exists, and it depicts the real world, then consider using a Classification Structure.

Finally, examine the model for derived results—e.g., "customer's age" in a system that already remembers the customer's date of birth. In a model of essential requirements, derived results muddy the picture. Gathering interim calculation results is a design decision; the requirement is most succinctly stated as the ability to do a calculation as if from scratch each time. Eventually the design team can add derived Objects (and add the Services governing immediate, periodic, or on-demand calculation) for performance considerations. For example, consider a problem space with actual drivers' licenses, along with many other printed reports. Avoid making each printed report an Object; such reports are somewhat arbitrary packages of essential and non-essential data. You may want to consider the content of existing reports, to see what Objects that the data might describe. For example, driver's license is a derived report, using information about a "Driver" Object (a role played) and a "License" Object (a legal event remembered); these two Objects are what is needed in the requirements model. So, don't make derived results Objects; instead, capture the data in Objects from which such derived results can be obtained.

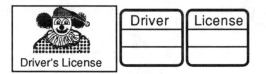

Figure 3.15: *Derived Results*

Thus, challenge unneeded remembrance/Services, single occurrences, and derived results.

3.3.5   How to Name Objects

Use a singular noun, or adjective+noun. An Object name should describe a single occurrence of the Object—e.g., when each occurrence describes something that gets shipped, use "Shipment Item" (each occurrence is one item) rather than "Shipment" (which seems like an entire truckload or plane load).

Choose Object names using standard vocabulary for the subject matter. Stick with names the user is comfortable with. As we learned on an air traffic control system, switching to more semantically accurate terminology only frustrates the client. We replaced terms such as "Minimum Safe Altitude Warning" with "Aircraft-to-Airspace Conflict Alert," a "better" description of what was being described. Each time we used our terms, we could almost see the client mapping them into more familiar terminology. And every time he spoke, he used his terms, along with "or whatever it is you're calling it." Lesson learned: stick to standard vocabulary for the subject matter.

Use readable names. Everyday upper-case and lower-case conventions make names easier to read. Resist the urge to add prefix and suffix codes; they're a bother to read and troublesome when they change midstream. Sometimes prefixes are added to help group related names together for lists. But this convention is not needed here. Attributes and Services are named with an Object name, followed by a dot, followed by the specific name.

Hence, use a singular noun or adjective+noun. Describe a single occurrence. Choose a name with the standard vocabulary for the subject matter.

3.4 KEY POINTS

Summarizing the "Identifying Objects" step:

Notation

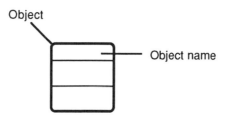

Strategy

Object = an abstraction of data and exclusive processing on that data, reflecting the capabilities of a system to keep information about or interact with something in the real world.

—Where to look: problem space, text, and pictures.

—What to look for: structure, other systems, devices, events remembered, roles played, locations, and organizational units.

—What to consider: needed remembrance, needed Services, more than one Attribute, common Attributes, common Services, and essential requirements.

—What to challenge: unneeded remembrance or Service, single instances, and derived results.

—How to name: use a singular noun, or adjective+noun. Use a name that describes a single instance of an Object. Use standard subject matter vocabulary. Use readable names.

Example—Sensor

The example system monitors sensors and reports problem conditions.

Problem Statement

Each standard sensor can be described by its model (manufacturer and model number), initialization sequence (sent to the sensor to initialize it), conversion (scale factor, bias, or unit of measure), sampling interval, location, state (on, off, or standby), current value, and alarm threshold. In addition, critical sensors are described by tolerance (the tolerance of the sampling interval).

Observations

The model consists of one Object: a device (Sensor). Details will follow with each subsequent OOA step.

Example—Registration and Title

The registration and title example comes from practice, applying object-oriented approaches during the development of a registration and title system in the state of Texas.[2]

Problem Statement

The registration and title system maintains information on the following:

Organization (name, manager, address, and telephone)
Clerk (user name, authorization, begin date, and end date)
Owner (legal name, address, and telephone)
Title (number, ownership evidence, surrendered title, and fee)
Registration (date and time start, date and time end, plate [issuer, year, type, and number], sticker [year, type, and number], and fee)
Vehicle (number, year, make, model, body style, gross weight, number of passengers, diesel powered, color, cost, and mileage; plus
for trucks: temporary gross weight
for motorcycle: gross weight does not apply
for trailers: diesel powered and number of passengers does not apply
for travel trailer: body number and length)

---

[2] The requirements for such a system would probably be somewhat different in other states or countries.

Clerks are accountable for registrations and titles issued (plus the fees accepted). Each clerk belongs to an organizational unit (county, region, or headquarters).

The system issues registration renewal notices.

The system does not keep inventory on title forms, plates, or stickers.

Observations

The model at this point consists of six Objects. One is another system (Vehicle), two are events remembered (Title, Registration), two are roles played (Owner and Clerk), and one is an organizational unit (Organization). Details will follow with each subsequent OOA step.

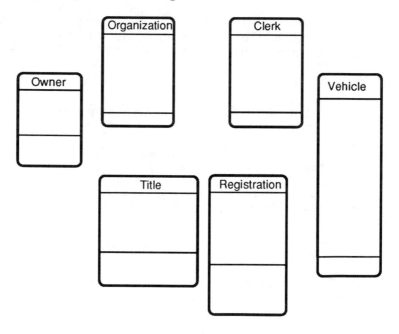

Example – Real-Time Airlift System

Another example is derived from an airlift system recently built in the U.S.

Problem Statement

The Real-Time Airlift System (RTAS) provides automated support to help Airlift Personnel expedite shipments of Passengers and Cargo Items. RTAS captures, maintains, and presents the following information:

Mission (code name, number, and description)
Flight (number, origin, and destination)
Passenger (name, rank, number, origin, destination, and now at)
Cargo Item (weight, dimensions, description, number, origin,
    destination, and now at)
Aircraft (call number, status, model, capacity, location)
Aircraft Failure (date and time, description, corrective action)
Radar (frequency, pulse interval, location, search space)

where origin, destination, and now at are described by date, time,
    and place.

In addition, RTAS provides radar search processing. RTAS provides aircraft tracking processing.

The system does not track valid origins or destinations. The system does not keep inventory on spare parts for aircraft repair.

Observations

Seven Objects are in the model. The Objects include other systems (Aircraft and Radar), events remembered (Mission, Flight, Cargo Item, and Aircraft Failure), and role played (Passenger). Details will follow with each subsequent OOA step.

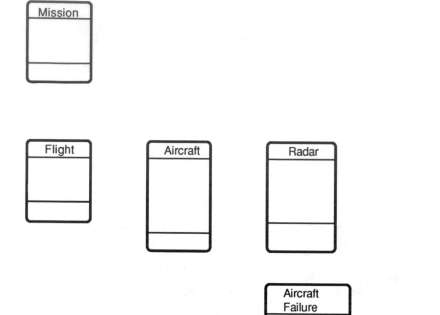

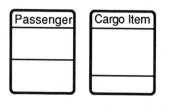

4 IDENTIFYING STRUCTURE

4.1 STRUCTURE—WHAT

Structures represent complexity in a problem space. Structures correspond to two of the three basic methods humans use to manage complexity. Classification Structure captures class-member organization. Assembly Structure portrays whole-part organization. Both types of structure are important components of the OOA approach.

4.2 CLASSIFICATION STRUCTURE—WHAT

Classification Structure helps depict a problem space class-member hierarchy. It shows generalization and specialization of real world things, with common characteristics and extension of those characteristics into specialized cases.

Transport

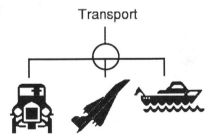

Figure 4.1: *A Classification Structure*

For example, consider the generalization Transport, and its specializations of Car, Aircraft, and Ship. Some Attributes and Services apply to all transports; others apply just to a Car, Aircraft, or Ship.

Classification Structure provides an important partitioning of a problem space. One partitioning consists of dividing Attributes and Services into mutually exclusive groupings. Another partitioning consists of using structure to identify a higher level of abstraction than Objects or Structure; this, the "Subject Layer," is covered in greater detail in a later OOA step.

Classification Structure also provides a "levelling" of information about a problem domain—putting Services and Attributes that are common at a higher level, and then extending the Services and Attributes to a lower level.

The concept of *inheritance* is an integral part of Classification Structure. Inheritance provides an explicit method for identifying and representing common Attributes and Services. Within a Classification Structure, inheritance makes it possible to share Attributes, share Services, add Attributes, and add or extend Services.

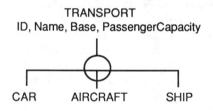

TRANSPORT
ID, Name, Base, PassengerCapacity

CAR   AIRCRAFT   SHIP

ID, Name, Base, PassengerCapacity

Figure 4.2: *Shared Attributes in a Classification Structure*

An Object shares the Attributes defined above it in a Classification Structure. For example, consider an occurrence of a car within the transport structure. It shares the Attributes defined for all Transports—e.g., ID, Name, and Base. Note that the common Attributes are shown only once within a Structure (and will be specified only once).

TRANSPORT
ID, Name, Base, PassengerCapacity
GetName

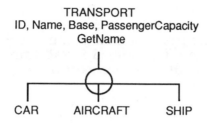

CAR   AIRCRAFT   SHIP

ID, Name, Base, PassengerCapacity
GetName

Figure 4.3: *Shared Services in a Classification Structure*

An Object shares the Services defined above it in a Classification Structure. For example, an occurrence of a car within the transport structure shares the Services defined for *all* Transports. Note that the common Services appear once within the Structure (and will be specified only once).

TRANSPORT

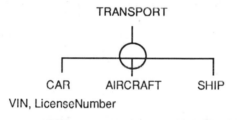

CAR   AIRCRAFT   SHIP

VIN, LicenseNumber

ID, Name, Base, Passenger Capacity

VIN, LicenseNumber

Figure 4.4: *Adding Attributes to a Classification Structure*

An Object represented by a Classification Structure can add to its inherited Attributes, extending the generalization above it in the Structure. For example, an occurrence of a car not only has the Attributes defined for all transports, but also those Attributes particular to each occurrence of car.

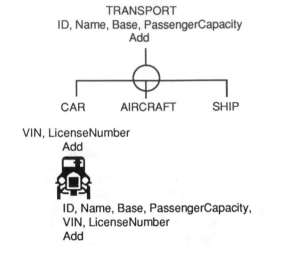

Figure 4.5: *Extending Attributes in a Classification Structure*

To add or extend Services, an Object represented by a Classification Structure can add to or extend its inherited Services, extending the generalization above it in the Structure.

4.3 ASSEMBLY STRUCTURE—WHAT

An Assembly Structure portrays a whole and its component parts. For example, an automobile consists of engine, transmission, and brakes.

4.4 CLASSIFICATION STRUCTURE—WHY

Classification Structure expresses a basic human method of organization. "Most practical activities, whether on an individual or social level, involve classification." [Britannica]

With Classification Structure, analysts gain leverage from the explicit capture of commonality—of Attributes and of Services.

4.5 ASSEMBLY STRUCTURE—WHY

Assembly Structure expresses a basic method of human organization, the natural whole-and-parts structure, thus modeling the aggregation of parts into an assembly.

4.6 STRUCTURE—HOW TO DEFINE

Examine each Object (even while identifying Objects) for Classification Structure and Assembly Structure.

4.7 CLASSIFICATION STRUCTURE— HOW TO DEFINE

Consider an Object as a generalization, look at different specialization possibilities in the problem space. Can the specializations of the Object be described with different Attributes, Services, or both? Does the specialization reflect meaningful real-world specialization? Is the specialization within the problem space (i.e., are the specialized Attributes and Services within the scope of the system under consideration)?

Aircraft

Figure 4.6: *Defining a Classification Structure*

For example, consider the Object "Aircraft." It could be specialized into a variety of specialized classifications:

- Civilian and Military

- Jet and Airplane

- Fixed Wing and Moveable Wing

- Commercial and Private

- En Route and On Ground.

In each case, look at the potential Attributes and Services. Does a distinction between the specializations exist? Also, check to be sure it's a real-world specialization; one wouldn't make "Car" a specialization of "Aircraft," even though conceivably some of the Attributes might be common. Also consider whether or not the specialization is in the problem space, e.g., does the system under consideration care whether an aircraft is fixed wing or moveable wing?

As another example, consider the Object "Radar." It could be specialized into Continuous Wave and Pulsed-Doppler. The Attributes and Services that apply to both kinds of radars belong in the generalization; the extension of the capability belongs in the specialization.

Next, consider an Object as a specialization. Do other problem space Objects fit into a generalization, expressing common Attributes, Services, or both? Does the generalization reflect a real-world generalization (or are you trying to force a Structure that does not reflect problem space, just because two Objects seem to have an Attribute or two in common)? Is the generalization itself in the problem space, i.e., within the scope of this system?

Figure 4.7: *Generalizing Objects*

For example, one could look at "Truck" and "Car" Objects, and generalize into Vehicle.

As another example, look at "Cargo" and "Passenger" Objects and generalize them into Shipment Items. This example reflects a real-world structure. And, common Attributes and Services fit into Shipment Item (e.g., origin, destination, and current location). For this example, the structure is within the problem space under consideration, so the structure belongs in the model.

As a contrasting example, notice that a number of Objects can have a common Attribute, e.g., "Location." Yet unless that Attribute describes some problem space generalization, we should not add a contrived Classification Structure just for the sake of capturing that commonality. The structure must reflect real-world structure. Structure is used in the model because it is one of the three basic human methods of organization; a consequence of such structure however is that commonality may be explicitly captured.

Add the Classification Structure, drawing general-to-specific, top-to-bottom. When reading a Classification Structure, an instance of a structure may be thought of as a "slice" out of the structure. For example, an instance of the Classification Structure Radar in Figure 4.8 is either a Continuous Wave Radar or a Pulsed-Doppler Radar—but not just a Radar all by itself.[1]

Place Attributes and Services in the Classification Structure, using inheritance to explicitly express commonality of Attributes and Services. Position the common Attributes in the parent and put the specialized Attributes in the children. Place the common Services in the parent and put the specialized Services in the children.

---

[1] For OOPLs, an abstract class corresponds to a generalization in a Classification Structure.

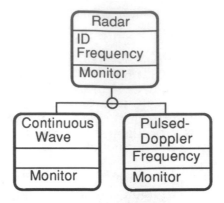

Figure 4.8: *Common Attributes*

4.8 ASSEMBLY STRUCTURE—HOW TO DEFINE

Consider each Object as an assembly. What are its parts or components? Does the system need to keep track of each occurrence of a part? Can each occurrence of a part be described with Attributes? Do parts reflect real-world parts? Is a part within the scope of the system under study?

Jet Engines? Avionics? Tires?

Figure 4.9: *Defining an Assembly Structure*

For example, an aircraft consists of engines, avionics system(s), tires, seats, and other parts. Within an engine maintenance problem space, perhaps the only component that the system needs to keep information about are engines. So consider an "Engine" Object. Be sure that each occurrence can be described with Attributes (e.g., ID, manufacturer number, model number, serial number, installation date, and latest service date). Check that the parts do indeed reflect real-world aircraft components. Thus, for engine maintenance, this Assembly Structure is within the scope of the system under consideration.

Consider each Object as a part. What assemblies does the Object fit into? What other Objects combine with this Object to form an assembly (of components into a whole, or perhaps people into an organization)? Does the system need to keep track of each occurrence of the assembly? Does the assembly reflect a real-world assembly? Is the assembly within the problem space?

County

Figure 4.10: *Combining Objects Into Assemblies*

For example, consider a clerk in the context of a registration and title system. The clerk fits into a greater whole, as a worker at a county, a region, or at headquarters. The assembly can be called "Organizational Unit" or simply "Unit," where each occurrence of the assembly maps to some number of occurrences of Clerk, and each occurrence of Clerk maps to one occurrence of the assembly.

In this case, the system needs to keep track of each occurrence of the assembly. The Assembly Structure reflects real-world aggregation. And yes, it is within the problem space (the system will need to know what Clerk occurrences correspond to an occurrence of a Unit, to support features such as end-of-day summaries and month-to-date queries).

Add Assembly Structure, drawing whole-to-parts, top-to-bottom. Use a single bar to show a single part; use crows' feet to show multiple parts. Put a single bar near the assembly when a part can occur only in one assembly (this case is the norm); use a "crow's-foot" otherwise (this notation will be further explained and expanded in Chapter 6).

4.9 KEY POINTS

Summarizing the "Identifying Structure" step:

Notation

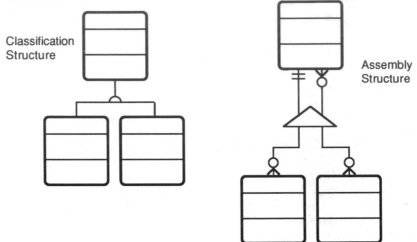

Classification Structure

Assembly Structure

Strategy

Structure = representation of complexity in a problem space.

Classification Structure represents class-member organization, reflecting generalization-specialization. Assembly Structure represents aggregation, reflecting whole and component parts.

Classification Structure. Consider each Object as a generalization, then as a specialization.

Assembly Structure. Consider each Object as a whole, then as a component part.

Checks: real-world structure, within the problem space, and within scope.

Example—Sensor

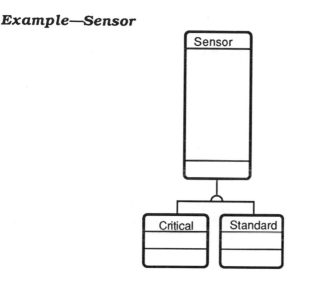

The sensor system has one Classification Structure, reflecting the two kinds of sensors: Critical and Standard.

The registration and title system has two Classification Structures and one Assembly Structure.

Two earlier Objects (Title and Registration) have been generalized, forming a legal Classification Structure.

One earlier Object (Vehicle) has been specialized with different kinds of vehicles (Passenger, Truck, Motorcycle, and Trailer); Trailer is further specialized into Standard Trailer and Travel Trailer.

Two earlier Objects (Organization and Unit) have been connected to reflect an Assembly Structure. The triangle points to the assembly; the markings indicate instance constraints between participating Objects; an Organization can be present without assigned Clerk(s); and, a Clerk can be present only when assigned to one (and only one) Organization.

Example—Registration and Title

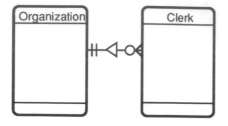

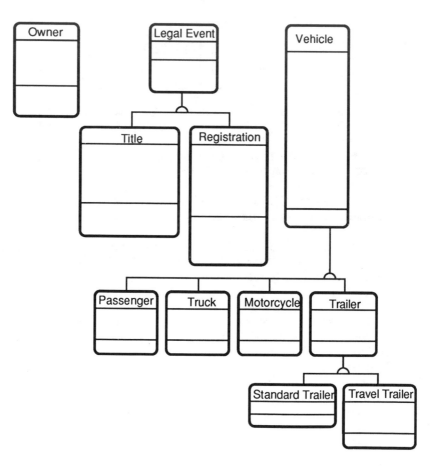

Example—Real-Time Airlift System

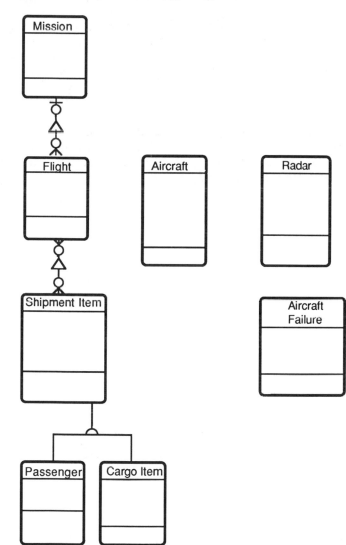

The real-time airlift system has one Classification Structure and two Assembly Structures.

Two Objects previously identified have been generalized, forming the "Shipment Item" Classification Structure.

Two earlier Objects (Mission and Flight) have been connected to reflect an Assembly Structure. The triangle points to the assembly; the markings indicate instance constraints between the participating Objects; a Mission can exist without any Flight(s) assigned, a Flight can exist without any Missions, and a Flight is part of at most one Mission.

"Flight" and "Shipment Item" also reflect an assembly and component part. The end markings indicate that the assembly and its parts can exist independently or as related in any quantity as whole and parts.

5   IDENTIFYING SUBJECTS

5.1   SUBJECTS—WHAT

Subjects provide mechanisms for controlling how much of a
model a reader (analyst, manager, or customer) is able to
consider and comprehend at one time. Subjects also give an
overview of the diagrams in the OOA model.

The primary basis for identifying Subjects is the
problem space structure identified with Classification and
Assembly Structures. Such structures are pervading methods
of organization used by humans—a very strong basis for
developing Subjects.

5.2   SUBJECTS—WHY

Real systems have a substantial number of Objects and
Structures. For example, the registration and title system
discussed in this book (mostly a data management problem)
has about 35 Objects (depending on scope); a full-scale air
traffic control system like the kind described in this book has
several hundred Objects. Yet, one of the critical success
factors for any method and its application is its ability to
facilitate communication, avoiding analyst and client
information overload.

Efforts to provide abstractions in the software
engineering field have been heavily influenced by George
Miller's infamous paper, "The magical number seven, plus or
minus two: Some limits on our capacity for processing

information" (*Psychological Review*, March 1956, pp. 81-97). Miller reported that human short-term memory seems to be limited to about 5-9 things at a time (unless a person has been taught to use linked list memory tricks).

Miller's results can be interpreted in different ways. One interpretation is that we *control visibility* to make a system model understandable to the human reader. This control can be accomplished by putting a 7 ± 2 limit on the number of items (or "icons," or "objects") that we show on a single drawing. Classical structured analysis approaches, such as those popularized in Tom DeMarco's *Structured Analysis and System Specification* (Prentice Hall, 1979), frequently took this approach. Indeed, certain CASE tools even *enforce* such a guideline. Ugh!

Yet this guideline is a particular interpretation of the "7 ± 2" rule. Its consequence is the need for many diagrams and many *levels* of diagrams. In larger systems, this need poses a problem—the reader must digest all of the pictorial summaries to understand the textual specifications at the bottom level. This interpretation of Miller's concept controls how much a reader sees at one time—but the detriment is wading through the levels. For a complex, real-world system, the burden is placed upon the reader to wade through a hierarchy of diagrams; only the bottom-most ones are described with text.

Another interpretation of Miller's work is to *guide reader attention.* This phrase means guiding the reader through a large diagram, using groupings on the diagram to help lead the reader from one area of "7 ± 2" components to another. This approach is taken by Chris Gane and Trish Sarson in their book, *Structured Systems Analysis: Tools and Techniques* (Improved Systems Technologies, 1977). This interpretation means fewer pieces of paper and fewer levels in the hierarchy. For a system modeled with data flow diagrams, this approach might result in a top-level context diagram with just one or two large diagrams below it. The lower diagrams might be as large as a full 11- x 17-inch sheet of paper—but parts of the diagram are grouped together to guide the reader's attention to different parts of the model.

So, the amount of complexity confronted by the reader *is* controlled, but not with a vertical stack of diagrams.

Effective analysts package information concisely. Miller's work gives us a guideline for such packaging. In OOA, we apply Miller's concept in two ways: control visibility *and* guide reader attention. First, we *control visibility* by controlling the number of layers visible to the analyst or customer. The Objects, Structures, Attributes, Connections, and Services can be freely turned on and off at will. For example, the reader may choose to look only at the Object and Structure Layers, reviewing and refining the model at that level of abstraction. Later, the reader may want to consider only Objects, Structures, and Attributes. And so the work can proceed at any level of abstraction.

We also apply Miller's concept by *guiding reader attention.* OOA adds a Subject Layer, which presents the overall model from an even higher perspective. The Subject Layer helps a reader review the model, succinctly summarizing the Subjects within the problem space under consideration.

5.3 SUBJECTS—HOW TO DEFINE

To select Subjects:

Add a Subject corresponding to each Structure.

Add a Subject corresponding to each Object.

If the number of Subjects exceeds 7 or so, then refine the Subjects further. Once Connections between Objects and Structures are identified during the Attribute and Service steps, combine tightly coupled Subjects, as needed, to provide a better overview (road map) for the reader to follow.

To construct the Subject Layer:

Show Subjects and Message Connections between Subjects on the Subject Layer.

Number the Subjects. Show the Subjects on the Layer diagrams to guide the reader from Subject-to-Subject. As needed to facilitate communication, each layer may be organized into diagrams separated by Subject.

Draw the Subjects as simple rectangular boxes with appropriate names. Do not show the Attributes (or subordinate Structures) on the Subject Layer diagram. An example is shown in Figure 5.1.

For example, a Classification Structure, possibly together with connecting Objects or other Structures, would be grouped into a Subject. Specifically, the Classification Structure "Vehicle" is grouped into a Subject in the Subject Layer, as shown in Figure 5.1.

Connections are shown on the Subject Layer, reflecting all of the connections of the Subject with other Subjects. The Subjects are then reflected when viewing other model layers, using Subject partitioning lines on a single, larger diagram, or for larger models by using separate diagrams, organized by Subject.

OOA applies Miller's "7 ± 2" rule by *controlling visibility* and *guiding reader attention*. The result is five layers, providing five levels of abstraction: Subject, Object, Structure, Attribute, Connection, and Service.

So when should Subjects get introduced into the model? It depends upon the model complexity itself. On very small projects, a Subject Layer may not be needed at all (the other Layers are simple enough as is).

For projects with up to several dozen Objects, the Objects and Structures can be identified first, and then the Subjects as a means of guiding the reader through the model.

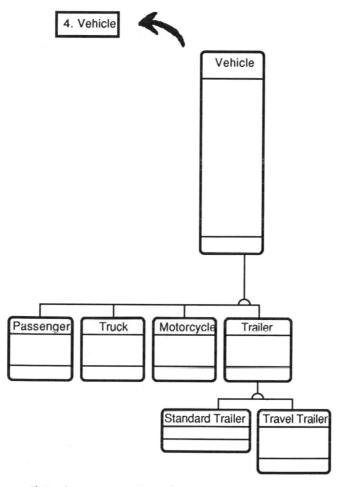

Figure 5.1: *Grouping a Classification Structure into a Subject*

But very large projects need Subjects right away. In this case, we recommend that a team of senior analysts do a rapid first-pass identification of Objects and Structure, and then identify an initial set of Subjects; such a rapid first-pass is sometimes called a "blitz." These Subjects can be assigned to teams. Later, the Subjects can be revisited and fine-tuned, based upon further system understanding of Structures (as described in this chapter) and Connections (as described in the next two chapters).

5.4 KEY POINTS

Summarizing the "Defining Subjects" step:

Notation

Subject

```
┌─────────────┐
│             │
└─────────────┘
```

Strategy

Subject = a mechanism for controlling how much of a model that a reader considers at one time.

Add a Subject corresponding to each Structure. Add a Subject corresponding to each Object.

If the number of Subjects exceeds 7 or so, then refine the Subjects further. Once Connections between Objects and Structures are identified during the Attribute and Service steps, combine tightly-coupled Subjects, as needed, to provide a better overview (road map) for the reader to follow.

Show Subjects and Message Connections between Subjects on the Subject Layer.

Number the Subjects. Show the Subjects on Layer diagrams to guide the reader from Subject-to-Subject. As needed to facilitate communication, each layer may be organized into diagrams separated by Subject.

Example—Sensor

The sensor system has no need for a higher-level overview to guide the reader, so no Subject Layer is needed.

Example—Registration and Title

The Subjects for the registration and title system reflect two underlying Classification Structures (Legal Event and Vehicle) and one Assembly Structure (Organization with its Clerks).

Example—Real-Time Airlift System

The Subjects for the real-time airlift system reflect the underlying, closely interconnected structures as the Mission Subject.

6 DEFINING ATTRIBUTES

6.1 ATTRIBUTES—WHAT

Attributes are data elements used to describe an instance of an Object or Classification Structure.

Name
Address
Title

Figure 6.1: *Attributes*

For example, consider a human being who plays a role of interest to the system under consideration. What attributes of that human being should the system keep track of?

For an Object called "User," the problem space dictates the appropriate Attributes. This implication means that we have a new opportunity to discuss system context with the user—in other words, how much data about users should be kept? What Services need to be provided?

Some Attributes are fairly straightforward—name, address, and title, perhaps. But of course, many more Attributes are possible for a "User" object. For example, both authors travel around the country and the world on consulting assignments at a pace that most humans would consider unusual, if not downright insane. One of the authors recently used his credit card in a part of the world he had not previously traveled to (when in Beijing, does one use Diner's Club or American Express at the restaurant? In Tbilisi, is MasterCard or Visa the best way to get a cash advance?). In a matter of days, his credit card company sent him a form letter saying, "By the way, we noticed your card being used in a place we're not used to seeing it used. Is everything OK? Is your card stolen?"

This concern indicated that their system was keeping track of information and providing processing about us (in our roles as Users) that we don't believe is any of their business. Eventually, they could monitor the fact that we buy flowers on the opposite side of town from where we live, and try to make some sort of conclusions. Some invasion of privacy issues may apply here. Nonetheless, the analyst who developed that credit card system had to decide what Attributes were needed for the system to meet its desired objectives.

Another example is an "Aircraft" Object. What detailed information must be captured for each instance of an aircraft that the system must have knowledge of?

Our system model is now getting more specific and more detailed. Objects are described by Attributes, which are further described in the Object Repository. With Attributes, we become more specific about problem space abstractions (Objects and Structures) in the OOA model.

6.2 ATTRIBUTES—WHY

Attributes clarify what is meant by the name of an Object, by adding more detail about the abstraction being modeled.

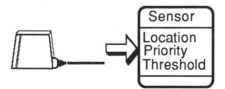

Figure 6.2: *Providing Details with Attributes*

Choosing Attributes involves analysis and choice. For a "Sensor" Object, the analyst makes a conscious choice in detailing the abstraction. For example, sensor weight and color, while pertinent in other contexts, are not part of the more detailed abstraction chosen in the example. Instead, location, priority, and threshold represent *in this system* in more detail what is meant by the abstraction "sensor"; Services will use the location, processing priority, and monitoring threshold, producing an alarm when the threshold is exceeded.

Attributes describe information that will be hidden in an Object, to be exclusively manipulated by the Services of that Object. We treat Attributes and exclusive Services on those Attributes as an intrinsic whole. If another part of the system needs to get information out of an Object, it will do so by specifying a message, corresponding to a Service defined in the Object. So, information hiding and data abstraction come into play as we move along in the OOA method.

Note that over time, the problem space Objects remain quite stable. However, Attributes within Objects are more likely to change. For example, consider an "Aircraft" Object within air traffic control. At the time this book was written in the late 1980s, an aircraft could transmit its identification and altitude. But several years from now, aircraft may be able to report rate of climb/descent, the position of each flap, and the status of each on-board system; the system on the ground may know when an aircraft is turning, rather than having to solely guess (extrapolate) with radar, as is done today. The "Aircraft" Object will remain the same, but the number of Attributes (and exclusive Services on those Attributes) will change.

6.3 ATTRIBUTES—HOW TO DEFINE

Define Attributes by applying the following steps:

Identify the Attributes.
Position the Attributes.
Identify and Define Instance Connections.

Revise Objects.
Specify the Attributes and Instance Connection
    Constraints.

6.3.1   Identify the Attributes

To begin, the analyst must return to the subject matter, and ask, "What Attributes apply to each instance of this Object or Classification Structure?" This step requires returning to problem space descriptions and interacting with the user.

Attach each Attribute to the problem space Object or Classification Structure that corresponds to the real-world thing that the Attribute most closely describes. In most cases, this correspondence is fairly straightforward—e.g., a vehicle has the Attributes VIN and Beijing. But when it's a close call—i.e., when it's not clear which Object should get a particular Attribute—look back at the problem space itself. Which Object does the Attribute *really* describe? Model the reality. The rationale: maximum stability and modeling consistency.

For example, in an automobile registration and title system, the system may know about vehicle color (at least once a statute is passed allowing for such information to be kept—law enforcement organizations would like this feature very much!). But where does the Attribute "color" belong? Vehicle color is going to be captured at the time the vehicle is registered. Does this addition mean that "color" describes a registration event or does it describe a vehicle? Color really is descriptive of a vehicle (it's painted a particular color)—even though the information is captured at registration time. So the Attribute "color" describes an instance of a vehicle.

Identify each Attribute at the level of atomic concept. This concept may be an individual data element—e.g., driver's license number, or it may be a natural grouping of data elements—e.g., name (the composite of first name, middle initial, and last name) or address (the composite of street, city, state, mailing code, and country). The motivation for expressing an "atomic concept" is to produce a simpler model for human review, with fewer Attribute names, and natural data groupings for easier assimilation; the reader focuses on the fact that an Address is captured, rather than scanning the list of Attributes to determine if each part is somewhere in the list of Attributes. "Name" and "address" better represent what is being captured.

Deferred to design are the compromises between introducing new tables to eliminate data redundancy (normalization) vs. achieving acceptable performance. For design, normalization requires that each data element have no internal structure (this rule is part of putting data into first normal form). But, this normalization is not the analyst's concern as he builds the initial model. Indeed, at this early stage, there is no realistic way of knowing whether the designer will choose to normalize the data—and if so, what level of normalization will be achieved.

6.3.2   Position the Attributes

Position the Attributes, using inheritance in Classification Structures. If a generalization/specialization exists, put the common Attributes higher in the structure, and show the specialization below. If an Attribute applies to a majority of specializations, put it in the generalization, then override it for the specializations that do not need it. An example is shown in Figure 6.3.

The "x" notation indicates that an inherited Attribute does not apply to a particular specialization or its subordinates.

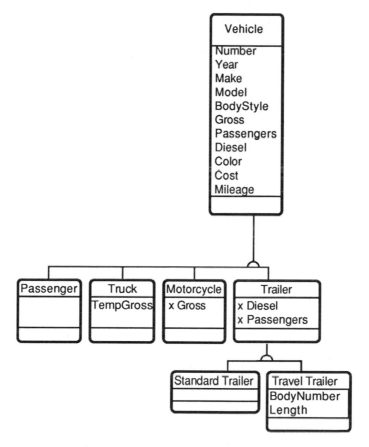

Figure 6.3: *Positioning the Attributes*

Remember that the model needs to reflect problem space understanding. And that communication is the key issue in applying any software method. We have chosen Attribute override over multiple inheritance as a better means of representing problem space structure.[1]

---

[1] Multiple inheritance is a feature found in certain OOPLs (notably C++ version 2.0 and later). Multiple inheritance means that a class can inherit variables (Attributes) and methods (Services) from more than one parent. This capability gives extra power in pulling out commonality, maximizing code reuse. However, the net effect is a cumbersome model that in practice obscures the actual problem space structure. Since our concern in OOA lies first with an accurate model of the problem space, we have elected to

If you find a situation where an Attribute sometimes has a meaningful value, but sometimes is "not applicable," consider Classification Structure. For example, if you have identified an Attribute "pregnancy," and then discover that it simply does not apply to some instances of your "User" Object, it's a clue that you need to classify users into male and female.

6.3.3   Identify Instance Connections

An Instance Connection is a mapping from the one instance to another.

Identifying and defining Instance Connections can be done in four steps:

1. Add Instance Connection lines.
2. Define multiplicity.
3. Define participation.
4. Check for special cases.

First, add the Instance Connection lines.[2] Draw lines to reflect the problem space connections between instances of Objects. Limit the connections to those of interest in the problem domain—i.e., show only those Instance mappings that need to be supported by the system. For example, Figure 6.4 shows a mapping of the instance of "Owner" to an instance of "Legal Event" (title and registration), and a mapping of an instance of "Legal Event" to an instance of "Vehicle." Clerks are held accountable for each legal instance they add to the system, so an Instance Connection line is shown between "Clerk" and "Legal Event."

---

[1] (continued) capture commonality with single inheritance, and minimize redundancy across specializations by allowing a generally applicable Attribute to be specified higher and then overridden lower, within the specializations that do not need the Attribute. Moreover, such an override could be applied to Services as well, although we do not apply such an override in Chapter 7.
[2] It's OK to add a label to the line if you feel the added understandability compensates for the added notation. This is not a religious issue; we have simply seen too little benefit from the labels to warrant using them.

So why not draw a direct connection between "Owner" and "Vehicle"? We are looking for a minimalist set of connection lines; every Instance Connection line implies a corresponding Message Connection Line, because an instance on one side needs to send a message to an instance on the other side whenever an implicit connection identifier is modified. In this example, if an instance of "Legal" must always occur (i.e., has mandatory participation) between an "Owner" and a "Vehicle," the connection between "Owner" and "Vehicle" is implicitly included in the model.

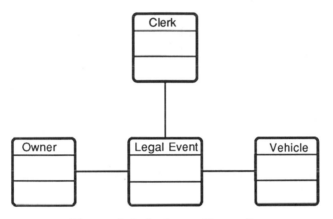

Figure 6.4: *Instance Connections*

An Instance Connection represents a simple mapping associating the instance(s) of one Object or Structure with the instance(s) of another. The underlying semantics of the association is not as strong as that of an Assembly Structure (where assembly and component parts is one of the basic methods of organization that pervades all peoples' thinking). Yet the association is significant nonetheless; here, it captures the connection between owner Coad and his purchase of a particular Jaguar (ah, wishful thinking...).

Connect Objects at an upper level if appropriate; for example, "Owner" would connect at the generalization of "Legal." Connect to a Classification Structure's specialization(s) when a connection does not apply to all specializations. For example, a "Smog Check" Object would connect at the specializations of "Vehicle" for which smog checks are applicable: car and truck, but not trailer.

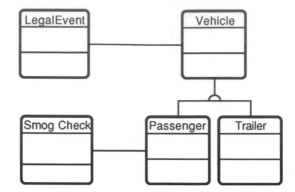

Figure 6.5: *Connecting Generalizations and Specializations*

The second step is to define multiplicity. For each direction of an Instance Connection line, consider the multiplicity by asking the following question:

For each direction, is the Instance Connection between the Objects

- *a single connection (1:1), or*
- *a collection of connections (1:M)?*

Add a single (vertical) bar to show a 1:1 connection and a crow's foot to show a 1:M connection. For example, Figure 6.6 shows that a single instance of "Owner" may map to some number of "Legal" instances—potentially a collection of connections.

A single "Legal" instance may map back to some number of owners (e.g., a purchase mapping back to co-purchasers). A single "Legal" instance maps to one instance of "Vehicle" and one "Clerk" (clerks are held accountable for the legal events they record).

A single instance of "Vehicle" may map to some number of instances of "Legal" (a potentially large number of legal events recording purchases, titles, and registrations).

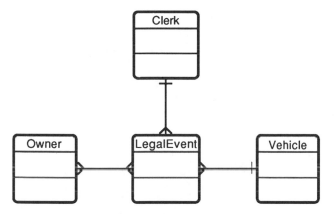

Figure 6.6: *Defining Multiplicity*

For an analyst and customer, establishing these instance mappings and constraints explicitly brings out many exceptions—e.g., that more than one owner can legally own a single vehicle. Detailed nuances are brought into the open, and significant problem space details are discovered. Such attention to detail provides vital information for identifying and defining Services in the next major step of OOA.

After drawing the connection lines and adding multiplicity, the next step is to define participation. Ask this question: For each direction, is the Instance Connection between Objects mandatory or optional? That is, does it make sense for an instance of one Object to exist without a corresponding instance of another Object? Or, must the connection be present?

Add a single bar for mandatory connections and add the letter "o" for optional connections. For example, the connections between owner, legal, and vehicle are mandatory. These connections indicate that for an instance of "Owner," corresponding instance(s) of "Legal," "Vehicle," and "Clerk" must be present. It makes no sense for this system to know about an instance of "Owner" without also knowing about these other instances. This requirement places constraints across multiple Objects that must be established and maintained by Services.

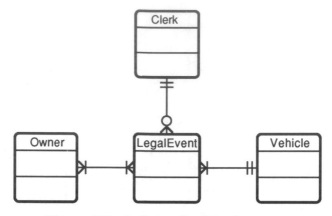

Figure 6.7: *Defining Participation*

An instance of "Clerk," may or may not have a connection to some number of "Legal" instances. The connection is not required; an instance for a new clerk can be added, even though that clerk might not be allowed to perform official legal events for awhile.

Now you may find that you prefer to combine these last two steps, and think directly in terms of 0:1, 1:1, 0:M, and 1:M mappings. The notation on the following diagram reflects this idea quite well:

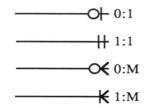

This conceptualization combines both multiplicity and participation. If you are more comfortable as an analyst with that terminology, then combine the two steps. In examining problem space, we prefer two distinct steps, focusing on one at a time.

In our experience, clients and users invariably find that the two-step approach is more effective—focusing first on the number of potential connections, and then establishing whether such a connection is required or not. This separation keeps the semantics underlying the representation clearer.

The final step is to check for special cases. Four common types of special cases exist:

1. Connections across three or more Objects or Classification Structures.

2. Many-to-many Instance Connections.

3. Instance Connections between instances of the same Object or Classification Structure.

4. Multiple Instance Connections between two Objects or Classification Structures.

6.3.3.1 Connections across three or more Objects or Classification Structures.

When one or more connections are optional, it may be necessary to add additional Instance Connections. If Instance Connections are required, then no additional connections are needed because the various mappings between Objects are required as well. In the previous example, "Owner" and "Legal" had a mandatory Instance Connection, and "Legal" and "Vehicle" had a mandatory connection. The mapping between "Owner" and "Vehicle" (by means of "Legal") is required to be present.

But, what if Instance Connections between three or more Objects is optional in one or both directions? For example, in Figure 6.8 below, observe that an instance of "Owner" must map to an instance of "Legal."

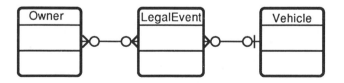

Figure 6.8: *Optional Instance Connections between Three Objects*

Can an instance of "Owner" and an instance of "Vehicle" be present without connections of each to an instance of "Legal?" For example, does the system need to keep track of owners whose vehicles were purchased and registered out-of-state? If so, then don't make assumptions about such a connection existing via "Legal"; instead, add an explicit Instance Connection between "Owner" and "Vehicle," as shown in Figure 6.9.

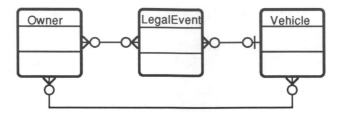

Figure 6.9: *Explicitly Showing Optional Connections with 3 Objects*

6.3.3.2 Many-to-many Instance Connections.

Many-to-many Instance Connections are perfectly fine in the model. At this point, examine each one for potential model refinement. For a many-to-many Instance Connection, check to see if some Attributes actually describe the connection (the mapping itself) between Objects. This redundancy means the Attributes really don't belong to one Object or the other, but actually describe the connection between them, when the two of them are connected. If so, then you've uncovered an Object that represents a "Thing Remembered," ready to add to the model.

Consider the following example. An analyst has modeled owner and vehicle. But certain Attributes describe the connection between the instance of these Objects: Date, Time, Amount, and Mileage. For example, one owner may purchase a vehicle at a particular date, time, amount, and mileage. A year later, another person may make a purchase of the same vehicle; a new date, time, amount, and mileage describes that purchase. Thus, Figure 6.10 shows a new "Thing Remembered" Object is uncovered: "Purchase."

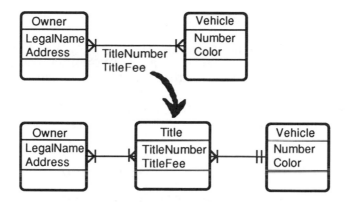

Figure 6.10: *Identifying a New Object*

When such an addition occurs, add a new Object and put the descriptive Attributes (plus a new "ID") into the new Object. Add multiplicity along with mandatory participation notation on the Instance Connection ends closest to the new Object. Then add the notations for the other participating Objects.

6.3.3.3 Instance Connections between instances of the same Object or Classification Structure.

An instance of an Object may have potential Instance Connections to other instances of the same Object. Check to see if the Instance Connection has descriptive Attributes. If not, use the connection alone (although this case seems fairly rare in real systems). If so, introduce a new Object to capture the Instance Connection.

For example, for a system with owners, in which co-ownership is needed but no other description of that ownership is needed, use one Object and a looping Instance Connection. For a counter-example, consider a system with owners, in which a number of Attributes about that ownership is needed, then both "Owner" and "Vehicle" Objects are needed within the model.

6.3.3.4 Multiple Instance Connections between two Objects.

When you discover more than one Instance Connection between two Objects, step back and consider the meaning of the two connections. Capture the underlying semantic distinction with one or more Attributes. Add the Attribute(s) to capture the distinction, and put just one Instance Connection between the two Objects on the model.[3]

The Services chapter will specify the processing required to support these instance mappings.

To recap, to define Instance Connections:

- Add Instance Connection lines.
- Define multiplicity.
- Define participation.
- Check for special cases.

6.3.4   Concerning Identification Attributes

Identification Attributes provide a convenient means of describing a single instance of an Object, plus connections to other instances.

Every Object and Classification Structure needs such identifiers. So as a convention, to keep the diagrams simpler, each Object and Classification Structure has an implicit identifier (oid, for "Object Identifier") and connection identifiers (cid, for "Connection Identifier(s)").

The primary reason for denoting these identifiers is convenience in specifying Object Services—i.e., to simplify describing an instance or a connection between instances.

Deferred to design is the actual choice of embedded keys, embedded pointers, correlation tables, or some combination thereof. As analysts, we want to avoid such

---

3   We prefer this approach, rather than labeling each line with active verb/passive verb pairs, a practice that clutters the model for little or no added client model understanding, and fails to address the need to capture the semantic distinction of different mappings with attribute(s).

design-dependent decisions. In the OOA model, we want each instance of an Object to be knowledgeable...and in this case, to know about its connections to other instances.

Another reason for using implicit Identifier Attributes is to avoid selecting "real-world" identifiers—ones the system is unable to issue directly—as unique identifiers. A unique identifier must be unique and not change once it is in the system. This isolation means making some design choices, because real-world identifiers cannot be guaranteed unique. For example, in an automobile registration system, Vehicle Identification Numbers (VINs) might appear to be unique. One could use VIN instead of "oid" for an instance identifier; but, real-world identifiers have duplicates. A clerk might enter an incorrect VIN number; some time later another clerk might try to enter the legitimate but duplicate of that number.

In Texas, for example, an individual can build his own trailer, put whatever VIN on it he desires, and get it registered. Moreover, that same individual can come in again with another trailer, with the same VIN on it (perhaps it has some special significance to him, like a winning lottery ticket number, or the date he graduated from college), and register that trailer too. So, even if manufacturers don't make mistakes (a bad assumption), the problem space still presents the potential for duplicate VINs.

Another example: in the United States, Social Security numbers seem unique enough, assuming we could ignore clerical errors (which is a bad assumption, because American Social Security numbers, unlike those in other countries, do not contain embedded check digits). And, because so many real-world systems *do* use Social Security number as an identifier, the typical analyst would assume that it's a safe choice—until he discovers that the numbers get recycled. Depending upon the problem space (e.g., a banking system), this potential duplication could be a serious problem.

Rather than use a real-world identifier (e.g., VIN) and a tie-breaker (e.g., VINTieBreaker) in analysis work—complicating the model and adding detail that is design-specific and possibly design-in-error—use the implicit identifiers ("oid" and "cid") as convenient "handles" for referring to instances of an Object. At design time, choose between a multi-Attribute key (real-world identifier plus a tie-breaker) versus a single Attribute key that can be guaranteed to be unique (one that the system itself generates).

Name each Attribute with a singular noun or adjective+noun.

Spell names out completely; avoid special codes: if it can't be pronounced, it can't be easily read; keep an on-line list of Attributes and abbreviations; strive for consistency.

6.3.5   Revise Objects

As you add Attributes, you may need to revise some Objects or Classification Structures. This section presents several checkpoints.

6.3.5.1 Attributes with values of "Not Applicable."

First, as mentioned much earlier in this chapter, if some Attributes do not apply to all instances of an Object or for a particular instance of a Classification Structure, then consider introducing additional Classification Structures.

6.3.5.2 Single Attributes.

Second, if an Object or an instance of a Classification Structure has only a single Attribute, then the model can be revised to reflect a higher level of abstraction. Move the single Attribute directly into the connecting Object(s) it describes, and remove the excess Object.

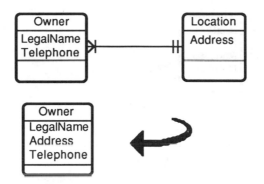

Figure 6.11: *Revising Initial Objects*

An example is shown in Figure 6.11 above. To control model complexity, we don't promote each Attribute to the stature of an Object; the model would explode from the loss of the Object → Attribute abstraction. Instead, we promote the higher level of abstraction (Owner) over a single Attribute (Location).

6.3.5.3 Repeated values for one or more Attributes.

The third refinement step involves looking for repeated Attribute values. If an Attribute of a single instance of an Object has potentially repeating values, consider adding a new Object. Do so only if the new Objects each qualify as Objects under the Object identification guidelines (i.e., don't add a new Object merely following data normalization principles). And do the resulting Objects each have more than one Attribute?

The new Object will have its own description Attribute(s); check for additional Attributes that apply to each instance of the new Object.

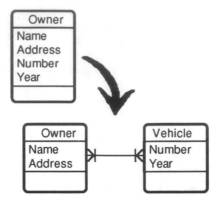

Figure 6.12: *Repeating Attribute Values*

An example is shown in Figure 6.12. The "Number" and "Year" Attributes have potentially repeating values. A "Vehicle" Object would qualify as an "other system" Object. And each of the resulting Objects has more than one Attribute.

6.3.5.4 Adaptation parameters.

Fourth, consider what should be done with adaptation parameters that have no home. For readers who build government systems, and especially those developed under DOD-STD-2167A, adaptation parameters are important. These parameters modify the overall processing of a system.

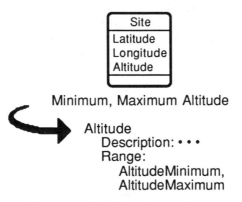

Figure 6.13: *Adaptation Parameters*

For installation-specific data, called installation adaptation data in DOD-STD-2167A, add a "Site" or "Location" Object, and put the installation Attributes in it. For operational ranges or limits set day-to-day, called operational adaptation data in DOD-STD-2167A, parameterize the corresponding range or limit Attribute descriptions within the Object Repository. An alternative for operational adaptation data is to make each range or limit an Attribute in its own right—but this alternative adds more Attributes to the model and to the descriptions in the Object Repository.

6.3.6   Specify Attributes

Specify Attributes with names and descriptions. Depending upon what helps to understand the description, or what's required by the customer, you may also add certain Attribute constraints (allowable values, range, limit, unit of measure, and/or precision). All such constraints are expected in many government standards (e.g., DOD-STD-2167A).

Also, identify which category that each Attribute falls into:

Descriptive - value is established and maintained by instance add, change, delete, and select.

Definition - value is potentially applicable to more than one instance of an Object or Classification Structure.

Always derivable - value is derivable from other data at any moment (and hence does not require its value to be held over time).

Occasionally derivable - value is derivable only occasionally (and hence a requirement to hold its value over time is needed).

For example, for the "Legal" Classification Structure:

descriptiveAttribute
 Legal.
   DateTime: the date and time of a legal transaction
   Title.
     Number: the officially recorded legal transaction number
     OwnershipEvidence: the proof of ownership provided
     SurrenderedTitle: the origin and number of the
       surrendered title.
   Registration.
     DateTimeStart: the starting date and time for the
       registration
     DateTimeEnd: the ending date and time for the registration
     Plate: the plate issuer, year, type, and number
     Sticker: the sticker year, type, and number

alwaysDerivableAttribute
 Legal.
   Title.Fee: the fee charged for a title
   Registration.Fee: the fee charged for a registration

instanceConnectionConstraint
   with Owner   1:M, required
   with Vehicle 1:1, required

And, for a "Sensor" Object:

descriptiveAttribute
Interval: the sampling interval for this sensor
Critical.Tolerance: the sampling interval tolerance for this
  sensor (if a critical sensor)
Location: the address for this sensor
State: the state of operation for this sensor (on, standby, or off)
Threshold: the alarm threshold value

definitionData
Model: the manufacturer and model number of a type of sensor
InitSequence: the initialization sequence for a type of sensor
Conversion: consists of scale factor, bias, and unit of measure

alwaysDerivableAttribute
Value: the current value of the Sensor, in actual units

6.3.7   Specify the Instance Connection Constraints

In addition, specify the Instance Connection constraints from
the perspective of one instance and its mapping constraints to
others.   Also include the mapping constraints due to any

Assembly Connections that an Object participates in as a whole or as a component part.

For example:

instanceConnectionConstraint
with Owner   1:M, required
with Vehicle 1:1, required

Note that this example refers to an *instance* of Legal Event.

6.4 KEY POINTS

Summarizing the "Defining Attributes" step:

Notation

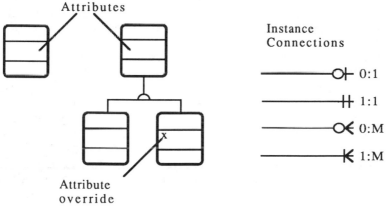

Attributes

Instance
Connections

———————O⊢ 0:1

———————|+ 1:1

———————O⪤ 0:M

———————⪤ 1:M

Attribute
override

Strategy

Attribute = a data element used to describe an instance of an Object or Classification Structure.

Identify the Attributes. Examine the problem space. Attach the real-world Object to the Attribute that actually describes it. Identify at the level of atomic concept an individual data element or a natural grouping of closely related data elements.

Position the Attributes. In a Classification Structure, position the common Attributes higher in the structure, and show the specialization below. If an Attribute applies to a majority of specializations, put it in the generalization; then, override it for the specializations that do not need it. If an Attribute at times could have the value "not applicable," look closely for an additional structure.

Identify and define Instance Connections. Add Instance Connection lines; reflect problem space mappings; strive for a minimal set of necessary connections; and, connect with a Classification Structure at the generalization level when the connection applies to all instances, otherwise only at the specific specializations. Define multiplicity: in each direction, establish a connection as a single connection or a collection of connections. Define participation: in each direction, define a connection as optional or mandatory. Check for special cases: connections across three or more Objects or Classification Structures, many-to-many instance connections, instance connections between instances of the same Object, and multiple instance connections between two Objects.

Revise Objects. Attributes with "not applicable" values imply another Classification Structure. Objects with a single Attribute imply that a higher level of abstraction is available. The Attribute should be placed inside of other Objects where it belongs. Repeated Attribute values may signal a new Object; check the Object identification guidelines; and, check that resulting Objects will each have more than one Attribute. Adaptation parameters become Attributes or minimum/ maximum parameters for the Attributes.

Specify Attributes by name, description, and the (optionally) allowable values of range, limit, unit of measure, and precision. Categorize each Attribute as descriptive, definition, always derivable, or occasionally derivable.

Specify Instance Connection constraints from the perspective of one instance and its mapping constraints with others. Also, specify the mapping constraints due to any Assembly Connections that an Object participates in as a whole or as a component part.

Example—Sensor

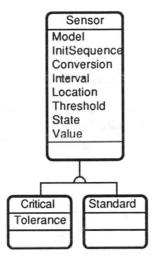

Note the inheritance in the Classification Structure. Each sensor is described by a common set of Attributes. Critical sensors inherit the common set of Attributes, and then extend it with "Tolerance." Standard sensors are described in full by the common set of Attributes that apply to all sensors.

Example—Registration and Title

Subject Layer:

Attribute Layer:

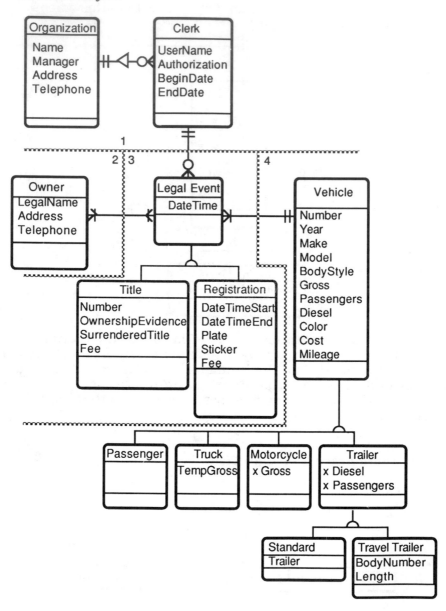

Note the inheritance of Attributes—the explicit representation of commonality—within the two Classification Structures, "Legal" and "Vehicle." Also note the Attribute overrides in the "Vehicle" Classification Structure.

The Instance Connections portray the multiplicity and participation constraints of this particular registration and title system.

Example—Real-Time Airlift System

Note the inheritance of Attributes within the "Shipment Item" Classification Structure.

The Instance Connection between "Radar" and "Aircraft" applies in a problem space with multiple aircraft, and the need to be able to know which radar's data were used in determining the position of an aircraft. The key point here is that the multiplicity and participation constraints are set by an interpretation of the problem space; the interpretation must be verified by problem space experts, with the client, or both.

Subject Layer:

Attribute Layer:

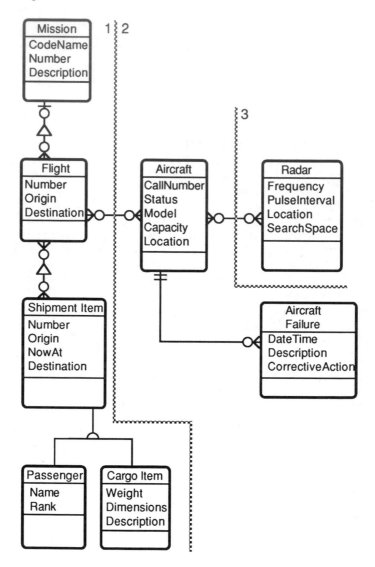

7 DEFINING SERVICES

One theme underlying object-oriented analysis is that eventually the analyst must provide a detailed description of a system's processing and sequencing requirements. These highly volatile subjects are recognized for their importance, yet deferred. Rather than jumping right into a study of functions and sequencing, the OOA analyst first focuses on Objects, Structures, Attributes (and Instance Connections)— and then finally gets around to a consideration of Services (and Message Connections).

7.1 SERVICES—WHAT

We define a Service as follows:

> a Service is the processing to be performed upon receipt of a message.

The central issue in defining Services is to define the required behavior for each Object and Classification Structure. Returning to Encyclopedia Britannica, the authors uncovered a classification scheme for behavior:

Three types of behavior classification are used most commonly:

(1) on the basis of immediate causation,
(2) on similarity of evolutionary history, and
(3) on the similarity of function.

Encyclopedia Britannica, "Animal Behaviour"

This three-part behavior classification corresponds to the strategies presented in this chapter for identifying Services:

Immediate Causation ➤ State-Event-Response
History ➤ Object Life History
Function ➤ Fundamental Services.

A second issue in defining Services is to define the necessary communication between Object instances. Message interaction corresponds to the imperative mood in languages. "The imperative mood conveys commands or requests...." [Encyclopedia Britannica, "Mood"]. Such commands and requests are the very nature of human interaction with a system. And the very same interaction paradigm is used between the Instances portrayed by the OOA model.

Services and Message Connections are specified in the OOA Repository, with a textual specification of the observable, measurable processing requirements.

Strategies for identifying Services and Message Connections, plus developing the corresponding textual specifications, are presented in this chapter.

7.2 SERVICES—WHY

Services further detail the abstraction of the reality being modeled, indicating what processing will be provided by an Object or Classification Structure.

Ultimately, every data processing system must have "data" and "processing." Our discussion in the previous chapter focused on the data in a system. Now we describe the functional processing that is to take place upon that data.

7.3 SERVICES—HOW TO DEFINE

The strategy for defining Services has four steps:

- Identify the Services (Primary Strategy)—this step gets Service names onto the diagram.

- Identify the Services (Secondary Strategies)—this step gets additional Service names onto the diagram.

- Identify the Message Connections—this step establishes inter-instance processing needs.

- Specify the Services—this step develops processing requirements.

7.3.1   Identify the Services—Primary Strategy

To identify the Services in a model, consider three fundamental Services for each Object or Classification Structure:

- Occur (instance add, change, delete, and select)

- Calculate

- Monitor.

These three fundamental Services provide a primary strategy for systematically identifying the specific Services in a system.

All OOA models utilize "Occur" Services. Some OOA models utilize "Calculate" Services, when one instance needs the processing results specified in another. And, some OOA models utilize "Monitor" Services, for the (usually small) part of the model that deals expressly with real-time processing (e.g., in air traffic control, Radar.Search and Aircraft.Track).

7.3.1.1   Occur.

The "Occur" Service establishes and maintains an instance of an Object or Classification Structure, with add, change, delete, and select. Each Object and Classification Structure requires an "Occur" Service. Rather than put the word "Occur" on each and every Object and Classification Structure on a diagram, the "Occur" Service is treated as an *implicit* Service:

- It is does not appear on the OOA diagram.

- It is specified once, as an implicit Service for all Objects and Classification Structures.

- It may be overridden by an Object or Classification Structure, when necessary.

A specification of the implicit "Occur" Service and an implicit Service override is presented later in this chapter.

7.3.1.2   Calculate.

A "Calculate" Service calculates results for an instance, or on behalf of another instance.

For example, in the registration and title system, two such Services are required: Registration.CalculateFee and Title.CalculateFee.

Note the use of a subject-specific Service name, rather than the generic term "Calculate."

Registration.CalculateFee is used by Registration.Occur (add, change, delete) and a Vehicle.Occur (change, delete). Title.CalculateFee is used by Title.Occur (add, change, delete) and Vehicle.Occur (change, delete). Vehicle.Occur uses these Services because a modification of vehicle attributes may have a fee impact (meaning more money may be due, or a refund may be in order).

Such a calculation may also be periodic in nature. Registration.CheckRenewals checks once per day for pending registration renewals, issuing renewal notices a parameter number of days prior to the expiration date.

When "Calculate" Services vary, add an appropriate Classification Structure to the diagram. When adding this Service to a Classification Structure, show a general "Calculate" Service higher, and specializations lower.

7.3.1.3 Monitor.

The "Monitor" Service performs on-going monitoring of an external system, device, or user. For example, if we have a "Sensor" Object in our model, a corresponding "Sensor.Monitor" Service and its specification would describe the on-going monitoring of the sensor, provided by an instance of a sensor.

For example:

Figure 7.1: *A Monitor Service*

The Services specification for Radar.Search would specify the on-going processing involved in searching a particular airspace for radar returns (called "targets"). Note that a subject-specific term should be used whenever possible, rather than literally using "Monitor."

Add such a Service for instances that must monitor another system or a device. When "Monitor" Services vary, add an appropriate Classification Structure. When adding this Service to a Classification Structure, show general "Monitor" Services higher, and specializations lower.

7.3.2 Identify the Services—Secondary Strategies

7.3.2.1 Object Life History.[1]

Object Life History portrays the events on an Object or Classification Structure over time.

The approach consists of:

- Define the basic Object Life History sequence.
- Check for variations on each step.
- Add to the basic sequence.
- Add Services.

Define the basic Object Life History sequence. To do so, begin by drawing a basic life sequence for an Object or Classification Structure:

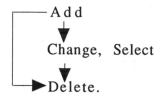

Check for variations on each step. Expand each step, showing variations of add, change, delete, and select.

For a clerk:

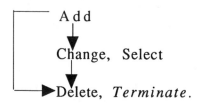

---

[1] Thanks to Mike Imber at LBMS in London for convincing one of the authors to investigate this strategy.

For a sensor:

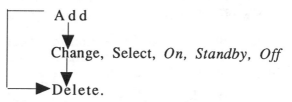

Add to the basic sequence. What other event does the Object or Classification Structure respond to?

For Legal.Registration:

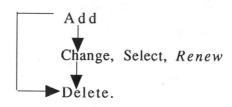

For a sensor:

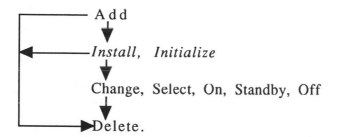

For a radar:

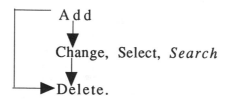

Add Services. Add to the fundamental Services as needed, so that the processing is defined for each step of the Object is life history.

For most Objects and Classification Structures, what you'll add are the variations within one or more of its fundamental Services. Yet, at times this secondary strategy will help you uncover additional "Calculate" or "Monitor" Services which otherwise might have been missed.

Document an Object's life history itself in the "objectLifeHistory" section of the specification template, described later in this chapter.

7.3.2.2 State-Event-Response.

Another secondary strategy is State-Event-Response. This strategy is used to discover additional Services for an Object or Classification Structure.

The strategy has the following steps:

- Define major system states.
- For each state, list the external events and required responses.
- Expand the Services (and Message Connections).

Define the major system states. What are the major states of behavior for the System? For example:

For a sensor system:
Off——Standby——Monitor.

For an air traffic control system:
Full Capability——Reduced Capability——Emergency.

For each state, list the external events and required responses. Put this information into a state-event-response table. We prefer a state-event-response table over a state-transition diagram (STD). An STD is little more than an extended flowchart. And like a flowchart, it gets rather ugly once it is applied beyond a small problem.

For an instance of a sensor:

State	Event	Response (action/new state)
Off	Add Command	Add/Off
Off	Initialize Command	Initialize/Standby
Standby	Monitor Command	Monitor/Monitor
Standby	Off Command	- /Off
Monitor	Threshold Exceeded	Monitor (report)/Monitor
Monitor	Standby	- /Standby
Monitor	Off	- /Off

For an instance of an aircraft:

State	Event	Response
Full	Communication Out	Track/Reduced
Reduced	Communication In	Track/Full
Reduced	Radar Out	- /Emergency
Emergency	Radar In	Track/Reduced

Expand the Services (and Message Connections) to provide the processing required in response to each event.

For a sensor, include both "Initialize" and "Monitor" Services. For aircraft, add Message Connections between "Aircraft" and "Radar," plus between the aircraft and communication systems.

This secondary strategy will help uncover additional "Calculate" or "Monitor" Services that might otherwise have been missed.

Document the state-event-response table in the "stateEventResponse" section of the specification template, described later in this chapter.

7.3.3   Identify Message Connections

A Message Connection combines event-response and data flow perspectives; that is, each Message Connection represents a message being sent, as well as a response being received. Message Connections are used to accommodate Service needs.

A Message Connection maps one instance with another, in which a "sender" sends a message to a "receiver," to get some processing done. The needed processing is named in the sender's Services specification, and is defined in the receiver's Services specification.

This convention is a specification discipline; literal messages of the "Hi, how are you doing?" variety are *not* sent from instance to instance. The benefit of such a discipline is that it creates a very narrow interface between the strong encapsulation of Attributes and exclusive Services on those Attributes, using Objects and Classification Structure.

When considering Message Connections, begin by adding Message Connections between Objects and Classification Structures already connected with Instance Connections. Also, examine the Objects and Classification Structures, together with the Attributes encapsulated in each, looking for Services needed by one instance to another—i.e., to get Attribute values for an instance, or to get some portion of processing done on the first one's behalf.

The graphical representation of a Message Connection is shown in Figure 7.2. The arrow represents a message, with the arrow's pointing from the sender to receiver.[2]

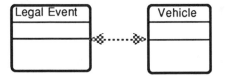

Figure 7.2: *Message Connections*

---

[2] It's OK to label the arrow if you feel that the added understandability warrants the added notation. This is not a religious issue; we have simply seen too little benefit from the labels to warrant using them.

An arrow, together with an arrow head, indicates that a Message Connection exists:

- The sender "sends" a message.
- The receiver "receives" the message.
- The receiver returns a response to the sender.[3]

Double-headed arrows show messages being sent from each participating Object or Classification Structure to the other. In Figure 7.2, the double-headed arrow between "Legal" and "Vehicle" reflects:

- the need for "Legal" to get instance values from "Legal" (needed in calculating fees).

- the need for "Vehicle" to get some processing done by "Legal" on "Vehicle's" behalf (a change in "Vehicle" requires a legal fee re-calculation).

Commands are the very nature of human interaction with a system. And the very same interaction paradigm is used between the instances portrayed by the OOA model. Human interaction could be shown on the model too, with message arrows going from the user to each Object and Classification Structure (as in Figure 7.3);

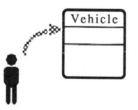

Figure 7.3: *Message Interaction Between User and System*

Additional arrows may be helpful when first introducing a client to a Subject layer. In other circumstances keep them off the diagrams.

---

[3] Note that this diagramming technique is much more than what is represented by a one-directional arrow in a data flow approach.

Document the Message Connection in the sender's Services specification; document the corresponding Service performed in the receiver's Services specification.

One might expect to find additional Message Connections when it comes time to document the details of all Services. Yet this first pass of Message Connections expresses many of the key processing dependencies between Objects or Classification Structures. This first pass can also be most helpful in systematically approaching the specification of Services for Objects or Classification Structures with such processing connections already in place.

7.3.4 Specify the Services

The specification of Services is presented in the following sections:

Focus on Required Externally Observable Behavior.
Use a Template.
Add Diagrams to Simplify Service Specifications.
Add Supporting Tables.
Develop Service Narratives—If You Must.
Put the Documentation Set Together.

7.3.4.1 Focus on required externally observable behavior.

Specify the required externally observable behavior for each instance. Each time, ask "Can this requirement be externally observed (tested)?" Consider writing a test for each requirement levied; this discipline helps streamline and focus requirements statements even further, emphasizing testable results and de-emphasizing processing steps, keeping the analyst from straying into over-specification.

Consider using a verb tense systematically, to give special emphasis to externally observable requirements. Moreover, such a discipline may be required contractually for Government system development.

Absolute tense: "shall"
> a binding, measurable requirement.

Future tense: "will"
> a reference to the future.

Present tense
> for all other verbs.

A "shall" requirement is observable when a system is delivered: observing the fulfillment of a requirement in terms of an end result (output) being produced by the system (e.g., shall output an alarm). Asking the question "Can this requirement be externally observed or tested?" is the key to accurately specifying such a requirement.

A "will" statement simply refers to the future, describing something that will happen, but is not under the control of the system being specified; typically these are human actions beyond system interaction (e.g., the controller will study the potential aircraft-to-aircraft conflict), or with independently developed systems (e.g., the independently developed radar system will report error conditions directly to the radar maintenance facility).

Use present tense in all other cases.

This verb tense discipline is applied in the examples presented in this chapter.

7.3.4.2 Use a template.

Use a template to develop bullet lists of requirements.[4]

> **specification** <Object name>
>
> **descriptiveAttribute** <...>
> **definitionData** <...>
> **alwaysDerivableAttribute** <...>
> **occasionallyDerivableAttribute** <...>

---

[4] This template was inspired by the crisp, clean syntax of the Ina Jo formal specification language [Wing and Nixon, 1989].

externalSystemInput <...>
externalSystemOutput <...>

instanceConnectionConstraint <...>

stateEventResponse <...>
objectLifeHistory <...>

notes <...>

intent/purpose <...>

service <...>

service <...>

service <...>

end specification

Where:

descriptiveAttribute Attribute(s) whose values are manipulated by Occur Services (add, change, delete, select). List Attribute constraints, as needed.
definitionData Attribute(s) whose values are potentially applicable to more than one instance of an Object or Classification.
alwaysDerivableAttribute Attribute(s) derivable at any moment (and hence no requirement to hold this data over time). List Attribute constraints, as needed.
occasionallyDerivableAttribute Attribute(s) derivable only occasionally (and hence a requirement to hold this data over time). List attribute constraints, as needed.

externalSystemInput input from a device or external system. List data constraints, as needed.
externalSystemOutput output to a device or external system. List data constraints, as needed.

instanceConnectionConstraint the Instance Connection constraint(s) for an instance

stateEventResponse the state-event-response(s) used in identifying Services
objectLifeHistory the Object Life History pattern used in identifying Services

notes analysis trade-off considerations

intent/purpose the purpose of the requirement

service the specification of a Service: a bullet list of
requirements, with one requirement per bullet

The template can be trimmed to suit specific project
needs. It may also be expanded, for in some system contexts
additional information may be needed for each Service, e.g.,

traceability the code(s) to trace back to a prior requirements
document (if any)
criticality the relative importance of the Service to the System
mission (if applicable)
budget the time and/or size estimate (if applicable)

As a first example of using a template, the implicit
"Occur" Service is specified by the following:

specification *implicit*

service Occur.Add
- will check the arguments against the corresponding Definition
Attribute constraints
- if a violation occurs, shall return an error report to the
Sender. End.
- will create a new instance.
- shall return the new oid (implicit Object identifier) to the
Sender. End.

service Occur.Change
- will check the arguments against the corresponding Definition
Attribute constraints
- if a violation occurs, shall return an error report to the
Sender. End.
- will check a cid (implicit Instance Connection identifier)
change against the corresponding Instance Connection
constraints
- if a violation occurs, shall return an error report to the
Sender. End.
- will change this instance. End.

service Occur.Delete
- will check the Instance Connection constraints
For each mandatory connection,
- shall output a delete message
- upon receipt of a response, if the deletion failed, shall return
an error report to the Sender. End.

For each optional connection,
- shall output a change message
- upon receipt of a response, if the change failed, shall return an error report to the Sender of the delete message. End.
Finally,
- will delete the instance. End.

service Occur.Select
-will check the selection criteria. If the criteria are not met, shall return <no match> to the Sender. End.
-will check that the Instance Connection constraints have been met (meaning that this instance has not only been added, but also that all of the required Instance Connections have been made)
- if the connection constraints are not yet met, shall return the values of this instance to the Sender, along with an Instance Connection constraint violation warning. End
- shall return the values of this instance to the Sender. End.

end specification

An implicit "Occur" Service is inherited by all Objects and Classification Structures. Yet at times some of these inherited Services may need to be overridden to meet special processing needs—and that's fine. For example:

specification Legal

definitionAttribute
Legal.
    DateTime: the date and time of a legal transaction
    Title.
        Number: the officially recorded legal transaction number
        OwnershipEvidence: the proof of ownership provided
        SurrenderedTitle: the origin and number of the
            surrendered title.
    Registration.
        DateTimeStart: the starting date and time for the
            registration
        DateTimeEnd: the ending date and time for the registration
        Plate: the plate issuer, year, type, and number
        Sticker: the sticker year, type, and number

alwaysDerivableAttribute
Legal.
    Title.Fee: the fee charged for a title
    Registration.Fee: the fee charged for a registration

instanceConnectionConstraint
    with Owner   1:M, required
    with Vehicle 1:1, required

service Registration.Occur.Add
- will check the arguments against the corresponding Attribute
  constraints
- if a violation occurs, shall return an error report to the
  Sender. End.
- will send the message Registration.CalculateFee
- shall output the fees to the Sender.

service Registration.AcceptFee
- precondition: immediately preceded by a no-error
Registration.Add
- if the precondition is not met, shall return an error report to
  the Sender. End.
- will create a new instance of Registration. End.

    • • •

end specification

Note that each instance is treated as an instance of Attribute values *and* corresponding processing. With the exception of "Occur Add" and "Definition.Occur" Services, each Service is specified in terms of the processing pertinent to a single instance. One outstanding Smalltalk designer and programmer, Sam Adams, of Knowledge Systems Corp., related to the authors that he designs and programs Objects by thinking in the first person (I receive a message. I check its arguments, and then I do the following calculations....). Sam even writes his implementation comments in first person. We think there is merit to such a thinking strategy in analysis, whether or not specifications could be written and delivered in this fashion would be largely a matter of organizational and customer desires.

A final example illustrates both definition data and the specification of interfaces with external systems (i.e., devices or other systems):

specification Sensor

descriptiveAttribute
Interval: the sampling interval for this sensor
Critical.Tolerance: the sampling interval tolerance for this
    sensor (if a critical sensor)
Location: the address for this sensor
State: the state of operation for this sensor (on, standby, or off)
Threshold: the alarm threshold value

definitionData
Model: the manufacturer and model number of a type of sensor
InitSequence: the initialization sequence for a type of sensor
Conversion: consists of scale factor, bias, and unit of measure

alwaysDerivableAttribute
Value: the current value of the Sensor, in actual units

externalSystemInput
    SensorReading: the raw data read from the sensor
externalSystemOutput
    SensorControl: the control command sent to the sensor

service Occur
-*implicit*, using the Descriptive Attributes

service Definition.Occur
-*implicit*, using the Definition Attributes

service Monitor
- shall output the InitSequence to the sensor at its Location
- will repeat with the current Attribute values for this sensor:
    - upon a change in InitSequence, shall output the InitSequence
      to the sensor at its Location
    - will sample the sensor at its Location, at the corresponding
      Interval
    - will convert the SensorReading into actual units with the
      equation:
          Value = (Bias * SensorReading) + Offset
    - if the Threshold value is met or exceeded, shall return an
      alarm to the Sender

service Critical.Monitor
extend
    - will sample the sensor at its Location, at the corresponding
      Interval, *within a tolerance of Tolerance*

end specification

7.3.4.3 Add diagrams to simplify Service specifications.

Most Service specifications will be well-structured and reasonably short. But a relatively small number of Services can benefit from added help in guiding the reader through the specification—e.g., Aircraft.Track. For these special cases, use pictures (block diagrams, data flow diagrams, and/or finite state machines) within the Service specification to guide the reader through the processing steps within a particular Service. For Aircraft.Track, a block diagram of the sub-steps is very effective.[5]

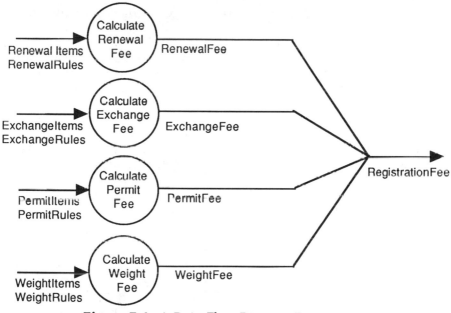

Figure 7.4: *A Data Flow Diagram Fragment*

---

[5]   Finally! We pull out of our tool kit none other than functional decomposition. And we recognize that procedural abstraction is one of the principles we can apply to manage complexity. In OOA, we accomplish this management in the limited scope of an Object, restricting the volatility to a limited part of the thinking and specification work. We find the Objects first, and then use whatever notations are most convenient for modeling those parts that OOA notation does not specifically prescribe, such as specific service modeling. This procedure contrasts with that of the "follow the flow"-OOD-modelers who propose to draw DFDs, STDs, and ERDs and *then* "find" the objects.

Another example of a special case is the calculation of registration fees. Fee calculation in Texas, for example, is very involved. To help guide the reader through the steps, a data flow diagram fragment is quite helpful, showing the progression of data flow and processing steps for this single Service; see Figure 7.4 above.

7.3.4.4 Add supporting tables.

Inter-Object dependencies are captured within a model with Message Connections. Yet when analyzing and specifying real-time systems, meeting stringent deadlines and repetition rates are central issues.

To summarize the interactions, especially for real-time system analysis and specification, utilize: (1) a summary of Services and applicable states;[6] (2) threads of execution analysis; and (3) timing and sizing budgets.

Services and Applicable States Table. Construct a Services and Applicable States Table. This table summarizes the state-dependent behavior in the OOA Repositories. For example:

	Full	Reduced	Emergency
Aircraft.Occur	•	•	•
Aircraft.Track	•		
Radar.Occur	•	•	
Radar.Search	•	•	

Critical Threads of Execution Analysis. Identify the state-event-response sequences that are vital to the system fulfilling its mission. This procedure includes identifying those events that have a corresponding hard, real-time

---

6   If the Service varies by system state, we could add a lower level of specialization, differentiated by state—e.g., Radar ... Full Capability Radar, and Reduced Capability Radar. But our preference is to model the actual problem space object (e.g., an external system called "Radar") and leave the state dependencies to an STD and text within the Services specification.

deadline (a hard deadline is one that must be met for the processing to be of any value to the system). For example,

>   State:
>   Full Service
>   Event:
>   Aircraft enters radar search airspace.
>   Response:
>   --->Radar.Search------>Aircraft.Track
>   - detect   - correlate
>   - report--->   - report--->

Timing and Sizing Analysis. Make estimates for each Service along a critical thread of execution. Add the estimates to come up with an overall thread estimate. For example,

>   --->Radar.Search--50 ms-->Aircraft.Track
>   - detect 1 s   - correlate 500 ms
>   - report 50 ms--->   - report 50 ms--->

Critical thread estimate: 1650 ms.

Revise the estimates as needed, working toward a final set of numbers. For example,

>   Budgeted time: 1550 ms
>   Revised estimates for each part:
>
>   --->Radar.Search--50 ms-->Aircraft.Track
>   - detect 1 s   - correlate 420 ms
>   - report 40 ms--->   - report 40 ms--->

Revised critical thread estimate: 1550 ms.

This entire example requires some assumptions as to how the design parts will interact with the available resources at run time. Simulation can make it possible to consider a wider variety of time budget estimates and implementation assumptions. But the challenge and guesswork of budgeting remain the same.

7.3.4.5 Develop service narratives—if you must.

Services specified with bullet lists keep the textual specification concise and well-focused. On the other hand, the reading audience (management, customers, and the like) may want to document system requirements in extensive narratives. Fight for bullet lists, they are succinct and drive home observable, measurable requirements.

If narrative text is required and/or desired, get technical writers—professionals with the prerequisite writing skills—to translate the bullets into narrative. Both the analysts and writers will be happier with their work assignments and the overall result.

If analysts are required to write narrative specifications, give them time to study *The Elements of Style* [Strunk and White, 1979] and *The Elements of Grammar* [Shertzer, 1986]. But listen to your staff; don't let them spend so much time in text refinement that they describe themselves as highly paid clerks (this sign is definitely a warning!).

Reduce the lard factor. The term "lard factor" comes from Lanham's *Revising Business Prose* [Lanham, 1981]. In his delightful book, Dr. Lanham gives practical advice on how to crush text down, squeezing the "official bureaucratese" out of the text. Lard factor is the percentage of wasted words to total words. A lard factor of over 50 percent is common for the uninitiated writer.

If your client believes that thicker specifications are better specifications, then perhaps you should do just the opposite of the following guidelines!

In any case, some key guidelines for reducing lard factor are:

1. Circle prepositions. Reduce the number of prepositional phrases that chain together (of the...in the...by means of the...).

2. Avoid "is"; the verb "to be" is the weakest verb (in English).

3. Use active voice: <subject><action verb><direct object>.

4. Use simple sentences (single subject, single action, single direct object).

5. Streamline introductions.

6. Read aloud, and delete the extras.

Key point: you needn't write in bureaucratese. And you needn't shift into passive voice.

However, your client may demand bureaucratese—e.g., to fulfill the documentation standards set by a government agency—but at least keep your technical work and thoughts clear. We have met analysts who not only wrote in bureaucratese, but also talked and thought in it. Ugh!

7.3.4.6 *Put the documentation set together.*

Finally, put the entire documentation set together. The full package contains:

- OOA Diagrams
  Subject, Object, Structure, Attribute, and Service layers.

- OOA Repository
  (one entry per Service or Classification Structure).

- Supporting Tables (if any).
  Services and Applicable States Table, Critical Threads of Execution Table, Timing and Sizing Table.

7.4 KEY POINTS

Summarizing the "Defining Services" step:

Notation

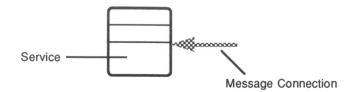

Service — [diagram] — Message Connection

Strategy

Service = the processing to be performed upon receipt of a message.

Identify Services. Primary strategy: fundamental Services—Occur (add, change, delete, and select), Calculate and Monitor. Secondary strategy #1: Object Life History—define the basic sequence, check for variations in each step, add steps, and add Services. Secondary strategy # 2: State-Event-Response—define the major system states, list the external events and required responses, and expand the Services and Message Connections.

Identify Message Connections. Add Message Connections for instances already connected by Instance Connections. Then examine processing needed by one instance from another, looking for additional Message Connections.

Specify Services. Focus on the required externally observable behavior. Use a template. Add diagrams to simplify the specifications. Develop narratives. Put the documentation set together.

A Specification Template

specification <Object name>

descriptiveAttribute <...>
definitionData <...>
alwaysDerivableAttribute <...>
occasionallyDerivableAttribute <...>

externalSystemInput <...>
externalSystemOutput <...>

instanceConnectionConstraint <...>

stateEventResponse <...>
objectLifeHistory <...>

notes <...>

service <...>

service <...>

service <...>

end specification

Where:

descriptiveAttribute Attribute(s) whose values are manipulated
by Occur Services (add, change, delete, select).
definitionData Attribute(s) whose values are potentially
applicable to more than one instance of an Object or
Classification Structure.
alwaysDerivableAttribute Attribute(s) derivable at any moment
(and hence no requirement to hold this data over time).
occasionallyDerivableAttribute Attribute(s) derivable only
occasionally (and hence a requirement to hold this data over
time).

externalSystemInput Input from a device or external system.
Constraints can be specified for these inputs, if applicable.
externalSystemOutput Output to a device or external system.
Constraints can be specified for these inputs, if applicable.

instanceConnectionConstraint The Instance Connection
constraint(s) for an instance.

stateEventResponse The state-event-response(s) used in identifying Services.

objectLifeHistory The Object Life History pattern used in identifying Services.

notes Analysis trade-off considerations.

intent/purpose The purpose of the requirement

service The specification of a Service: A bullet list of requirements, with one requirement per bullet

Example—Sensor

Service Layer:

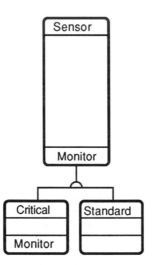

   Note the inheritance in the sensor's Classification Structure. Sensor.Monitor is defined for all sensors, explicitly capturing processing commonality. The processing is then specialized by Critical.Monitor. Also observe that no additional Attributes or Processing are needed for standard sensors.

Example—Registration and Title

Subject Layer:

Service Layer:

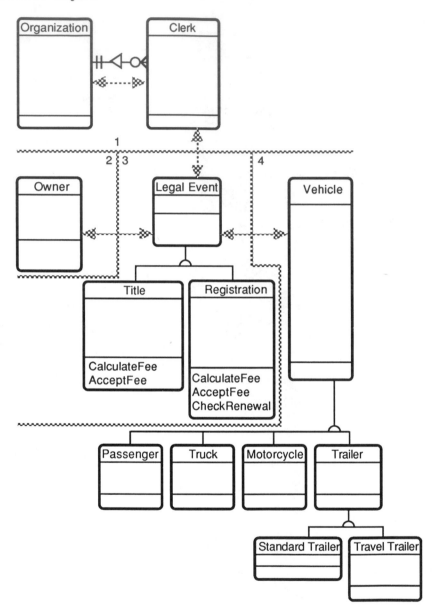

The "CalculateFee" and "AcceptFee" Services are entirely different. So no generalization of these Services is shown within "Legal."

Registration.CheckRenewal checks for registrations nearing expiration to issue renewal notices.

Example—Real-Time Airlift System

Subject Layer:

```
┌──────────┐        ┌──────────┐        ┌─────────┐
│1. Mission│ ◄──►  │2. Aircraft│ ◄──►  │3. Radar │
└──────────┘        └──────────┘        └─────────┘
```

Service Layer:

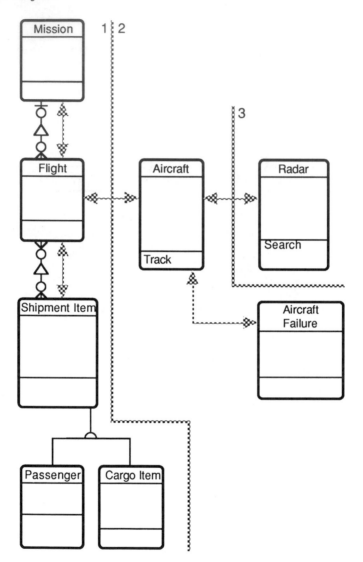

Note that the real-time flavor of this system is well-contained within a small portion of the overall model.

8 SELECTING CASE FOR OOA

8.1 CASE—AND SOME PUZZLING QUESTIONS

Computer-Aided Software Engineering (CASE)—it's hard to believe that such simplistic software tools are getting so much attention these days. The marketeers race to the drawing board, finding new ways to make their CASE product more provocative than the next.

Yet is it really CASE? The term "CASE" usually refers to limited graphics and text tools. Perhaps a less sexy but more accurate name would be CADC—Computer-Aided Drawing and Checking. This quieter acronym would go a long way in controlling your management's expectations of such products.

Why so little for (often) so much—in software cost, training cost, and support cost? Many tools consist of rigid graphics, simple text, rudimentary syntax checks, and a sub-standard human interface, at a surprisingly high price per copy.

Could drawing tools and a part-time clerk/diagram-checker be made more cost effective? Could such an approach reduce risk— in cost, schedule, and management aggravation?

Why are the tools hard-wired to a particular method (i.e., compliant with the DeMarco "Standard" (circa 1978) or the Coad/Yourdon "Standard" (circa 1990))? Why not allow the user to define his project's notations for nodes, connectors, connection rules, and the like—and then use the CASE tool he has defined in data?

Who uses CASE products? Is the human interface so tedious that the engineers pass red-lined documents to a clerk, to feed in the data? (If so, are only clerk copies needed?) Does the vendor sell a course just to teach someone how to use his product? (If so, just how poor is the human interface?)

For organizations that made a purchase, is the product still in use one year later? How much of it? What were the biggest problems? Did they find an automated work-around? Did it become shelfware?

8.2 EXPANDING CASE

CASE can be viewed in a much larger context than the hotly publicized tools of the present.   One would like to see automated assistance for the *entire* systems development life cycle, which involves over 100 functional capabilities; most commercially available products have a maximum of 20-30 such functional capabilities.[1]

8.3 WHAT'S NEEDED FOR OOA

CASE support for OOA requires the following:

8.3.1   Notation

Notation includes the following:

For the Subject layer—

- Subjects
- Message Connections.

---

[1]A representative list of CASE functions is discussed in "More on the Future of CASE," *American Programmer*, October 1988.

For the other layers—

- Subjects
- Objects
- Structures (Classification and Assembly)
- Attributes (and Instance Connections)
- Services (and Message Connections).

Graphic symbols are summarized in Appendix A.

8.3.2 Layers

Layer support needs to include on/off selection of the five OOA Layers (Subject, Object, Structure, Attribute, and Service).

8.3.3 Model Checks

Use model checks to get early warnings of errors, inconsistencies, and unnecessary complexity.

These checks may be done manually (with a checklist, by a clerk) or with the aid of a CASE tool for OOA. When automated, the checks should be project-definable as warnings (a rule that can be broken) or as errors (a rule that one is not allowed to violate).

For Objects:

- All Objects have names.

- All Objects have unique names.

- All Objects have two or more Attributes.

- All Attributes within a single Object have unique names.

- All Services for an Object have unique names.

- All Objects have at least one Instance Connection (this situation could happen; it's a warning).

- All Objects have at least one Message Connection.

For Classification Structures:

- All Classification Structure components (generalization and specializations) have names.

- All Classification Structure components have unique names.

- All Classification Structures (considered as a whole) have two or more Attributes.

- All Attributes in a Classification Structure component have unique names.

- All Attributes in a Classification Structure component have unique names within their ancestors and descendents.

- No Attribute in a Classification Structure appears in all specializations on a single specialization level.

- Overridden Attributes appear as regular Attributes in their ancestors in the Classification Structure.

- Overridden Attributes do not appear in their descendents in the Classification Structure.

- All Classification Structure levels must have at least one Attribute or Service.

- All Classification Structures have at least one Instance Connection.

- All Classification Structures have at least one Message Connection.

- Classification Structures with over three levels may be too complex (this situation could happen; it's a warning).

For Attribute definition and Service specification:

- Each Attribute in an Object or Classification Structure is defined and appears in a Service specification; each Attribute appears in the corresponding Object or Classification Structure.

- Each Object or Classification Structure has corresponding Services specified; each specified Service has a corresponding Object or Classification Structure.

- Each Service is defined in a corresponding Services specification; each Service mentioned in the Services specification (as a Service or Message name) has a corresponding Service on the diagram (excluding implicit Services).

- All external inputs/outputs defined in the Object Repository have unique names for the Object or Classification Structure.

- Each external input/output is defined; each external input/output appears in the Services specification.

For layers:

- The Subjects and Message Connections shown on the Subject Layer are consistent with other layers.

- Object, Structure, Attribute, and Service layers remain consistent with each other, descriptive of the same underlying model.

8.4 WHAT'S AVAILABLE

We use what we like to call "CardCASE."[2] It seems like a very promising—and extremely inexpensive—tool for object-oriented development. We use ordinary 3" x 5" index cards. We write the name of each potential Object and Classification Structure component on a separate card; next, we add Attributes. Then we put the cards on an 11" x 17" inch pad of paper (although a white board with magnets does nicely for larger systems). Finally we add Instance Connections, Services, and Message Connections. 3" x 5" index cards are *very* effective tools for OOA. They extract problem space understanding as we interact with our clients.

At the time of this writing, CASE vendors in a number of countries had expressed interest in supporting OOA, including Hewlett-Packard (Palo Alto, CA), Cadre Technologies (Providence, RI), Systematica (Bournemouth, England), CGI (Paris), Center for Industrial Research (Oslo, Norway), ISO (Munich, Germany), Knowledge Systems Corp. (Cary, NC) and LBMS (Houston and London). And, we expect that CASE support will be available from several additional vendors by the time this book is released.

8.5 ADDITIONAL CONSIDERATIONS

Many additional considerations come into play when evaluating and introducing CASE into a project. For this book, we'll stick to the OOA-specific requirements for CASE; however, the ideal OO-CASE tool will allow seamless integration of OOA, OOD, OO-implementation, and OO-testing.

For additional reading, refer to books and publications that focus on such matters, including *CASE Is Software Automation* (McClure, 1989) and *CASE: Using Software Development Tools* (Fisher, 1989).

---

[2] We developed this idea after hearing about Ward Cunningham (West Coast Software) and his "Cross Reference Cards."

9 MOVING TO OBJECT-ORIENTED DESIGN

9.1 ANALYSIS TO DESIGN

9.1.1 One Underlying Message

For requirements analysts, this chapter drives home one underlying message: moving from OOA to OOD is a progressive expansion of the model.

The OOA layers model the *problem space*. The OOD expansion of the OOA layers models a particular *implementation space*. The expansion primarily occurs with added Attributes and Services.

This expansion is in contrast to the radical movement from data flow diagrams to structure charts (or from data flow diagrams to an object-oriented representation). Such movement is abrupt and forever disjoint: designers get a hint from the analysis, and then go off to the "real" design. Such an approach fails to bring the requirements as a central issue into design. Moreover, traceability between the two is difficult and, in content, not very helpful.

9.1.2 Having It All: OOA to OOD to OO-DBMS

OOA is programming language-independent. Preliminary OOD remains largely language-independent. Detailed OOD is language-dependent, and can be effectively applied for procedural, package-oriented, and object-oriented programming languages.

Ideally, one would like a continuum of representation, from analysis to design to implementation: OOA to OOD to OO-DBMS (Object-Oriented Database Management Systems—the synergistic combination of an Object-Oriented Programming Language with a Relational Database Management System). In this case, OOA results are expanded into OOD results, which then map directly to OO-DBMS programming language and data management syntax.

9.1.3   Not Having It All: What to Do

What if you are caught somewhere in the development activities for a software system?

As an analyst.   OOA is programming language-independent.

The underlying principles—

Procedural Abstraction
Data Abstraction
Encapsulation
Inheritance
Communication Through Messages
Pervading Methods of Organization
     Objects and Attributes
     Classes and Members
     Whole and Parts
Behavior Categories
     Fundamental Functions
     State-Event-Response
     Object Life History

and model notations and strategies for establishing—

Objects
Classification Structures
Assembly Structures

Attributes
Instance Connections
Message Connections
Services

all work together to give the analyst effective thinking tools to get his job accomplished. No assumption is made about the design method or the programming language(s) that may be used to build the system.

As a designer. If you receive a non-OOA requirements specification, rapidly develop (say over 1-4 weeks) an OOA model, using the Services specifications to trace back to the functions in the supplied requirements specification. Resolve the holes you'll uncover along the way. Next apply preliminary OOD; then apply detailed OOD, aimed at the programming language(s) to be used for implementation.

As an implementer. If you receive a non-OOD, yet you plan on implementing the design using an OOPL or OODBMS, rapidly develop (1-4 weeks) an OOA model, and expand into an OOD model. Finally, apply detailed OOD, focusing on off-the-shelf classes and reusability.

Can you apply OOA and OOD, even though your organization mandates (by official policy or corporate culture) that all systems must be coded using fourth-generation languages (4GLs), or COBOL, or both? Yes. As Michael Millikin described it:

> Language battles aside, however, programmers can exploit object-oriented software design concepts even with traditional languages. [Millikin, 1989]

Language selection significantly affects the strategy and focus underlying OOD. Language selection also affects how much pre-defined syntax is available for expressing object-oriented constructions. Yet eventual implementation in a procedural or package-oriented language does not affect the effective use of OOA or OOD.

9.2 OOD AND HARDWARE ARCHITECTURE

OOD begins with expansion of the model according to the hardware architecture. With a centralized architecture, no expansion is needed at this point. For example, in a state-wide registration and title system, all Objects and Structures could be placed on one large computer. No additional detail is needed to reflect this design. With trade-off criteria, a designer can see if such a solution is acceptable, e.g., does it meet (weighted) the client needs of availability, response time, and timeliness of data?

With a distributed architecture, the designer chooses between replicated Objects and Structures versus distributed Objects and Structures. A replicated Object is one for which:

- the occurrences of an Object or Structure are duplicated (to some extent) on each processor.

- the Services of an Object or Structure are duplicated on each processor.

For example, consider the registration and title system again. This time, consider a distributed architecture: a large computer at headquarters, and fast but smaller processors in each county.

The designer could choose to replicate Objects and Structures on each processor. The only difference would be the number of occurrences at each site: each county processor would include the occurrences for that county; the headquarters processor would include statewide occurrences. Availability and response time may be improved, but at the expense of less timely data. And so the model (now an OOD model) needs expansion—a "Communication" Object, with an "Update" Service. This new Service specifies:

for outbound updating:
when to send messages to Objects and
Structures to gather changes

how they are packaged together
(with update type and update data)

how often an update is sent to other(s).

for inbound updating:
how the update is unpacked
(by update type and update data)

sending messages to update Objects
and Structures, accordingly.

With replicated Objects and Structures, availability and response time may be improved at the expense of less timely data. Note that the cost impact of replicated copies of processing is very significant unless the coding can be done once, and the different processors could be run without modification.

In contrast, the designer could choose to distribute the Objects and Structures on each processor. The designer's choices include the distribution of occurrences, the distribution of Services, or both. For example, for the registration and title system, the occurrences could be fully distributed: all occurrences pertinent to a county could be kept on the county processor, and not on any other. This setup gives the counties responsibility for their own data, at a cost of potentially poor performance at headquarters. Other considerations (e.g., how will backups be done?) must also be taken into account. Not only could the occurrences be distributed, but the processing could be distributed too. Some Services could be allocated to the large computer (due to performance or security reasons) alone.

And so the OOD model needs expansion—a "Communication" Object, with a "Request" Service. This new Service specifies:

for outbound requests:
receiving a request from an Object or Structure

> how the request is tagged and sent to another
> processor
>
> upon receipt of a response, how the response is
> unpacked (by response type and response data)
>
> sending a message to the requesting Object or
> Structure.

for inbound requests:
> upon receipt of a request,
>> how the request is unpacked (by request
>> type and request data)
>>
>> sending message(s) to fulfill the request.
>
> upon receipt of message response(s),
>> how the response is packed (by response
>> type and data)
>>
>> sending a response back to the sending
>> processor.

In practice, the designer may choose a design that replicates in part, and distributes in part. In this case, the OOD model is annotated to reflect these design decisions—alongside the upper right corner of the Object or Structure symbol, *r:<locations>* shows replication, and *d:<location>* shows distribution. If an Object or Structure is partially replicated and distributed, each Attribute and Service is annotated with this notation, to the right of each name in the symbol.

9.3 OOD AND SOFTWARE ARCHITECTURE

The designer now considers software architecture. Is concurrency or perceived concurrency of processing needed? Do the implementation language(s) support the concurrency implicitly (e.g., an object-oriented programming language?), explicitly (e.g., rendezvous in Ada?), or only by using operating system services?

Multiple tasks offer perceived concurrency, but at a price: added design complexity and performance considerations (context switch time from one task to the next to the next). Multiple tasks should be chosen judiciously, and justified with specific engineering criteria.

Select tasks by:

Start mechanism

Dependency on an input/output device

Response time

Computational intensity

Periodicity

Criticality.

A separate task diagram can show the tasks, priority, multiple instantiations, plus communication and coordination (via rendezvous, or with more traditional mailboxes, semaphores, and interrupts).

On the OOD model itself, indicate, off to the side of the lower right corner of an Object or Structure, the task name.

If the Services of an Object or Structure are partitioned into separate tasks, add the task indication next to each Service. If a Service is split into multiple tasks, expand the name of the Service into different names, identifying the Service to be done within each task.

If a manager task (e.g., a scheduler) is part of the task design, but does not fit within one of the OOD model's Objects or Structures, add a "Manager" Object (e.g., a "Scheduler" Object) to the OOD model.

Expand the Service specifications, adding inter-task communication and coordination.

9.4 CONTROLLING DATA REDUNDANCY

9.4.1   Mapping Attribute Values to Tables

In each Classification Structure, each component maps to a table, with the same identifier in each one.

Each Object becomes a table. Each Occurrence Connection may be designed as a table (consistent approach, one tool, but requires an extra table look-up to traverse the connection), as embedded foreign keys, or as embedded pointers.

9.4.2   Selecting Keys

A key must be an identifier under the system's control: it should be unique and never change. Real-world identifiers have duplicates (as discussed in Chapter 6). So, select a unique identifier generated by the system, or use a compound identifier (real-world identifier plus a tie-breaker).

9.4.3   Normalization: Reducing Data Redundancy at a Price

Normalization is a technique applied to data to reduce data redundancy and take fewer steps to modify the data consistently during an update or delete.

Yet this technique comes at a price too. The tables lose their 1:1 mapping with the Objects and Structures in the OOD model. And, the number of tables increases (hence, potentially impacting performance).

It is interesting to note that OOA results tend to be well on their way to being normalized; the underlying strategy of using the problem space to guide partitioning goes a long way in reducing data redundancy.

Normal forms provide a systematic approach to remove data redundancy.

1.   First normal form: each occurrence has exactly one value for each Attribute (no repetition, no holes); Attributes have no internal structure.

2.   Second normal form: (this issue applies only when a compound identifier is used) every non-identifier describes something identifiable only by the entire identifier, not just by part of the identifier.

3.   Each non-identifier depends on the key, and is not just a further description of another non-identifier.

4.   The values of two (or more) non-identifiers do not always map to the value of another non-identifier.

5.   The values of two or more non-identifiers following a join [a special relational operation] do not always map to another non-identifier.

OOA results tend to be well on their way to being normalized, and yet formal application of normalization is placed in design—when it's appropriate to consider each data element (no groupings allowed) and the appropriate tables. It's also in design that performance will dictate how far to carry normalization. Very rarely does full normal form meet performance requirements; a backing off (putting up with some data redundancy in exchange for fewer tables) comes into play.

9.4.4   Relational Database Management Systems

Relational database management systems (RDBMSs) provide an impressive array of tools for software development. And, their power is even further extended when coupled with an object-oriented programming language (a subject we'll pursue later in this chapter).

RDBMSs provide a data structuring based upon data attribute/data value pairs. No fixed ordering of Attributes is assumed. RDBMSs also provide support for data integrity: Attribute and domain integrity, unique identifier integrity, and referential integrity (interrelated occurrences are unambiguously related).

An RDBMS manipulates data with algebraic and relational operations. The basic algebraic operations are: union, intersection, difference, and product. The basic relational operations are: projection (extracts a table with only certain attributes), selection (extracts a table with only some occurrences), division (extracts a table of occurrences when two Attribute values from different tables match), and join (a product of the occurrences of different tables, followed by a selection to extract only some of the resulting occurrences).

9.5 OOD AND IMPLEMENTATION LANGUAGES

All languages permit Object-Oriented Programming (OOP). Some provide a much richer syntax for explicitly capturing the underlying representation used during OOA and OOD.

As Bjarne Stroustrup pointed out in "What Is Object-Oriented Programming:"

> A language is said to support a style of programming if it provides facilities that makes it convenient (reasonably easy, safe, and efficient) to use that style. [Stroustrup, 1988]

Let's return to the principles for managing complexity:

Procedural Abstraction
Data Abstraction
Encapsulation
Inheritance
Communication Through Messages
Pervading Methods of Organization
       Objects and Attributes
       Classes and Members

Whole and Parts
    Behavior Categories
        Fundamental Functions
        State-Event Response
        Object Life History

and examine the syntax support provided by four implementation language categories: procedural, package-oriented, Object-Oriented Programming Languages (OOPLs), and finally Object-Oriented Database Management Systems (OO-DBMSs).

9.5.1   OOD and Procedural Languages

For procedural languages (e.g., C, Pascal, FORTRAN, 4GLs, and COBOL), only procedural abstraction is directly supported by a language. Data abstraction and encapsulation can be added by style guides, programmer discipline, and team inspection "enforcement." (This discipline is in practice to some extent already, by designers applying structured design's information-hiding module.) Inheritance via classification cannot be explicitly shown; some of the commonality can be factored out into individual routines (with very limited possibilities for subsequent reuse). And, the pervading methods of organization have no explicit support. OOD leading to a procedural language is not technically gratifying, perhaps. Yet it does fit into a practical, viable approach: OOA to OOD to procedural language with OO-conventions. For some of our clients, this approach is exactly what is needed within the organization today (one author expects that one of his clients may be ready to proceed from procedural languages to OOPLs in about two decades—and that's an optimistic estimate!).

9.5.2   OOD and Package-Oriented Languages

For package-oriented languages (e.g., Ada), procedural abstraction, data abstraction, encapsulation, and one of the pervading methods of organization (Objects and Attributes) have direct syntax support. Inheritance via classification cannot be explicitly shown[1,2]; some of the other commonality can be factored out into individual routines (with very limited possibilities for subsequent reuse). Two of the pervading methods of organization (classes and members, and whole and parts) have no explicit representation. OOD leading to a package-oriented language is palatable, perhaps, and it presents a viable development approach: OOA to OOD to package-oriented language with OO-conventions. For our military and other real-time government system clients, this approach reflects exactly what will happen for many years to come.[3]

9.5.3   OOD and Object-Oriented Languages

Object-oriented languages (e.g., C++, Smalltalk, Objective-C, Actor, and Eiffel) directly support procedural abstraction (within a method), data abstraction, encapsulation, inheritance, plus two of the three pervading methods of organization (Objects and Attributes, and classes and members). Assemblies are not explicitly supported, but are conveniently expressed with composite objects. So OOA to OOD to OOPL presents an approach with a very consistent underlying representation.

An OOPL directly supports Message Connections, but not Occurrence Connections and Assembly Structures.

Using an OOPL, the designer takes on a fully different design focus. The designer considers a part of the design,

---

[1] Yes, genericity (type-independent parameters) is helpful, but it is no substitute for full inheritance.

[2] Software Productivity Solutions of Melbourne, Florida markets ClassicAda, a preprocessor that provides classes and run-time objects for Ada designers and programmers.

[3] The big payoff for the government in using a package-oriented language over a procedural language should be during maintenance! The richer syntax provides a means to express more of the design structure explicitly in the code. Automated tools can generate pictures of the design directly from the code; the team can review the picture of the design, knowing that it's up-to-date. In addition, explicit data abstraction makes it harder for a programmer to sneak in a routine to grab some data directly, rather than using Services that exclusively manipulate the data.

and then examines existing classes that are like or somewhat like that part of the design—meaning, it's close in its variables and methods. The designer then inherits that capability and extends it with sub-classes.

9.5.4   OOD and Object-Oriented DBMSs

An OO-DBMS is a combination of an OOPL with an RDBMS. But just as not all relational products are really relational, and just as not all object-oriented products are object-oriented, it's not too surprising that not all OO-DBMSs are necessarily "OO" or "DBMSs."

Four different architectures underlie the OO-DBMS field:

- Big attribute—an RDBMS is extended to allow big data attributes, e.g., a document. Example: Informix's "object-oriented" product.

- Loosely coupled—an OOPL and a number of possible DBMSs are combined. Example: Neuron Data's *Nexpert Object,* working with a number of commercial RDBMSs.

- Tightly-coupled—an OOPL and a specific data management system are offered as an integrated system. Example: Servio Logic's *GemStone.*

- Extended relational—an RDBMS is extended to allow data attributes of type "procedure." Example: Relational Technology's *Postgres.*

An OO-DBMS (loosely coupled, tightly coupled, and to some extent, extended relational) provides explicit syntax for each of the principles for managing complexity:

Procedural Abstraction
Data Abstraction
Encapsulation
Inheritance

Communication Through Messages
Pervading Methods of Organization
    Objects and Attributes
    Classes and Members
    Whole and Parts
Behavior Categories
    Fundamental Functions
    State-Event-Response
    Object Life History

9.6 WRAP UP

For requirements analysts, this chapter drives home one underlying message: moving from OOA to OOD is a progressive expansion of the model. The OOA layers model the *problem space*. The OOD expansion of the OOA layers model a particular *implementation space*. The expansion primarily occurs with added Attributes and Services.

Appendix A

KEY POINTS

A.1 CONCISE SUMMARY

This chapter presents a concise summary of OOA, with notation, strategy, and three examples.

A.2 IDENTIFYING OBJECTS

Notation

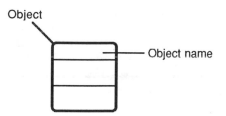

Strategy

Object = an abstraction of data and exclusive processing on that data, reflecting the capabilities of a system to keep information about or interact with something in the real world.

Where to look: problem space, text, and pictures.

What to look for: structure, other systems, devices, events remembered, roles played, locations, and organizational units.

What to consider: needed remembrance, needed Services, more than one Attribute, common Attributes, common Services, and essential requirements.

What to challenge: unneeded remembrance or Service, single instances, and derived results.

How to name: use a singular noun, or adjective+noun; use a name that describes a single instance of an Object; use the standard subject matter vocabulary; and use readable names.

Example—Sensor

The example system monitors sensors and reports problem conditions.

Problem Statement

Each standard sensor can be described by its model (manufacturer and model number), initialization sequence (sent to the sensor to initialize it), conversion (scale factor, bias, and unit of measure), sampling interval, location, state (on, off, or standby), current value, and alarm threshold. In addition, critical sensors are described by tolerance (the tolerance of the sampling interval).

Observations

The model consists of one Object: a device (Sensor). Details will follow with each subsequent OOA step.

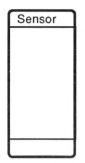

Example—Registration and Title

The registration and title example comes from practice, applying object-oriented approaches during the development of a registration and title system.

Problem Statement

The registration and title system maintains information on the following:

Organization (name, manager, address, telephone)
Clerk (user name, authorization, begin date, end date)
Owner (legal name, address, telephone)
Title (number, ownership evidence, surrendered title, fee)
Registration (date and time start, date and time end, plate [issuer, year, type, number], sticker [year, type, number], fee)
Vehicle (number, year, make, model, body style, gross weight, number of passengers, diesel powered, color, cost, mileage; plus
for trucks: temporary gross weight
for motorcycle: gross weight does not apply
for trailers: diesel powered and number of passengers does not apply
for travel trailer: body number and length).

Clerks are accountable for registrations and titles issued (plus the fees accepted). Each clerk belongs to an organizational unit (county, region, or headquarters).

The system issues registration renewal notices.

The system does not keep inventory on title forms, plates, or stickers.

Observations

The model at this point consists of six Objects. One is another system (Vehicle), two are events remembered (Title, Registration), two are roles played (Owner and Clerk), and one is an organizational unit (Organization). Details will follow with each subsequent OOA step.

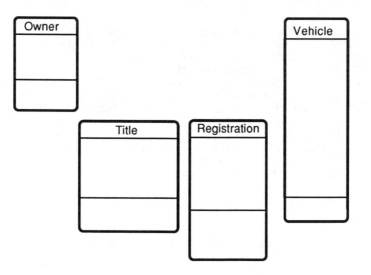

Example – Real-Time Airlift System

Another example is derived from an airlift system recently built in the U.S.

Problem Statement

The Real-Time Airlift System (RTAS) provides automated support to help airlift personnel expedite shipments of passengers and cargo items. RTAS captures, maintains, and presents the following information:

Mission (code name, number, and description)
Flight (number, origin, and destination)
Passenger (name, rank, number, origin, destination, and now at)
Cargo Item (weight, dimensions, description, number, origin, destination, and now at)

where origin, destination, and now at are described by date, time, and place.

In addition, RTAS provides radar search processing. RTAS provides aircraft tracking processing.

The system does not keep track of valid origins or destinations. The system does not keep inventory on spare parts for aircraft repair.

Observations

Seven Objects are in the model. The Objects include other systems (Aircraft and Radar), events remembered (Mission, Flight, Cargo Item, and Aircraft Failure), and role played (Passenger). Details will follow with each subsequent OOA step.

Mission

Flight

Aircraft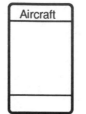

Radar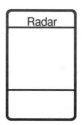

Aircraft
Failure

Passenger 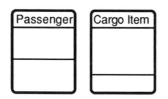 Cargo Item

A.3   IDENTIFYING   STRUCTURES

Notation

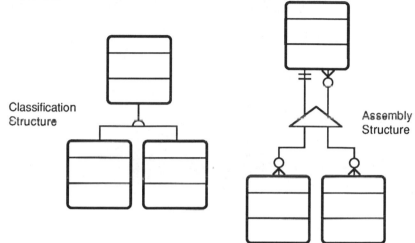

Classification Structure

Assembly Structure

Strategy

Structure = representation of complexity in a problem space. Classification Structure represents class-member organization, reflecting generalization-specialization.   Assembly Structure represents aggregation, reflecting whole and component parts.

Classification Structure: consider each Object as a generalization, then as a specialization.

Assembly Structure: consider each Object as a whole, then as a component part.

Checks: real world structure within the problem space, and within scope.

Example—Sensor

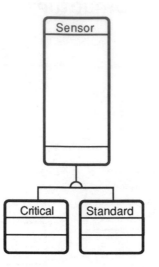

The sensor system has one Classification Structure, reflecting two kinds of sensors: Critical and Standard.

Example—Registration and Title

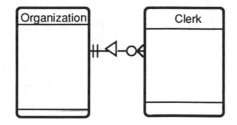

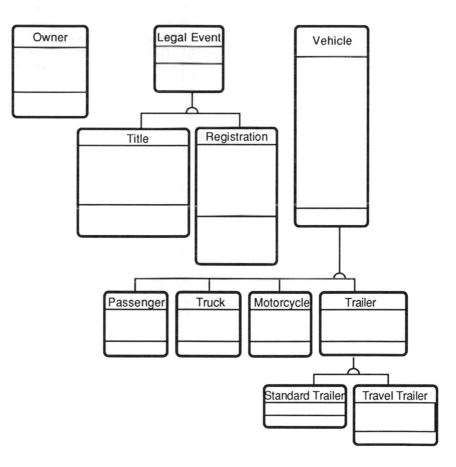

The registration and title system has two Classification Structures and one Assembly Structure.

Two earlier Objects (Title and Registration) have been generalized, forming the "Legal" Classification Structure.

One earlier Object (Vehicle) has been specialized with different kinds of vehicles (Passenger, Truck, Motorcycle, and Trailer); Trailer is further specialized into Standard Trailer and Travel Trailer.

Two earlier Objects (Organization and Unit) have been connected to reflect an Assembly Structure. The triangle points to the assembly; the markings indicate instance constraints between participating Objects; an Organization can be present without assigned Clerk(s); and, a Clerk can be present only when assigned to one (and only one) Organization.

Example – Real-Time Airlift System

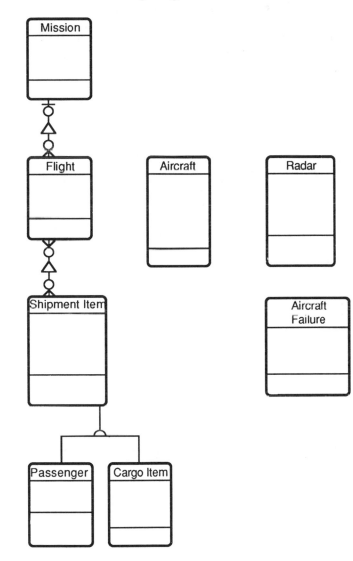

The real-time airlift system has one Classification Structure and two Assembly Structures.

Two Objects previously identified have been generalized, forming the "Shipment Item" Classification Structure.

Two earlier Objects (Mission and Flight) have been connected to reflect an Assembly Structure. The triangle points to the assembly; the markings indicate instance constraints between participating Objects; a Mission can exist without any flight(s) assigned, and a Flight can exist without any Missions (and a Flight is part of at most one Mission).

"Flight" and "Shipment Item" also reflect an assembly and component part. The end markings indicate that the assembly and its parts can exist independently or as related in any quantity as whole and parts.

A.4 IDENTIFYING SUBJECTS

Notation

Subject

Strategy

Subject = a mechanism for controlling how much of a model a reader considers at one time.

Add a Subject corresponding to each Structure. Add a Subject corresponding to each Object.

If the number of Subjects exceeds seven or so, refine the Subjects further: once the connections between Objects and Structures are identified during the Attribute and Service steps, combine tightly coupled Subjects, as needed, to provide a better overview (road map) for the reader to follow.

Show Subjects and Message Connections between Subjects on the Subject Layer.

Number the Subjects. Show the Subjects on the layer diagrams, to guide the reader from Subject-to-Subject. As needed to facilitate communication, each layer may be organized into diagrams separated by Subject.

Example—Sensor

The sensor system has no need for a higher-level overview to guide the reader, so no Subject layer is needed.

Example—Registration and Title

The Subjects for the registration and title system reflect two underlying Classification Structures (Legal Event and Vehicle) and one Assembly Structure (Organization with Clerks).

Example – Real-Time Airlift System

The Subjects for RTAS reflect the underlying, closely interconnected structures as the "Mission" Subject.

A.5 DEFINING ATTRIBUTES

Notation

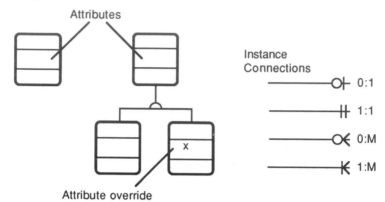

Strategy

Attribute = a data element used to describe an instance of an Object or Classification Structure.

Identify the Attributes: examine the problem space; attach the Attribute to the real-world Object that it actually describes; and identify at the level of atomic concept an individual data element or a natural grouping of closely related data elements.

Position the Attributes. In a Classification Structure, put the common Attributes higher in the structure, and show the specialization below. If an Attribute applies to the majority of specializations, put it in the generalization, then override it for the specializations that do not need it. If an Attribute at times could have the value "not applicable," look closely for an additional Structure.

Identify and define the Instance Connections: add Instance Connection lines; reflect problem space mappings; strive for a minimal set of necessary connections; connect with a Classification Structure at the generalization level when a connection applies to all instances, otherwise only at the specific specializations.

Define multiplicity: in each direction, establish the connection as a single connection or a collection of connections. Define participation: in each direction, define the connection as optional or mandatory. Check for special cases: connections across three or more Objects or Classification Structures, many-to-many Instance Connections, Instance Connections between instances of the same Object, and multiple Instance Connections between two Objects.

Revise Objects: Attributes with "not applicable" values imply another Classification Structure; Objects with a single Attribute imply that a higher level of abstraction is available, putting that Attribute inside of other Objects where it belongs; and repeated Attribute values may signal a new Object—check Object identification guidelines and check that the resulting Objects will each have more than one Attribute. Adaptation parameters become Attributes or minimum/maximum parameters for Attributes.

Specify Attributes: name, description, and the (optionally) allowable values, range, limit, and unit of measure, (precision). Categorize each Attribute as descriptive, definition, always derivable, or occasionally derivable.

Specify the Instance Connection constraints, from the perspective of one instance and its mapping constraints with others. Also specify mapping constraints due to any Assembly Connections that an Object participates in as a whole or component part.

Example—Sensor

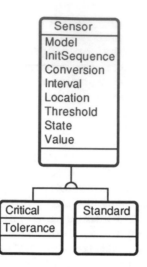

Note the inheritance in the Classification Structure. Each sensor is described by a common set of Attributes. Critical sensors inherit the common set of Attributes and then extend it with Tolerance. Standard sensors are described in full by the common set of Attributes that apply to all sensors.

Example—Registration and Title

Subject Layer:

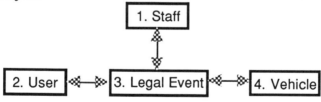

Attribute Layer:

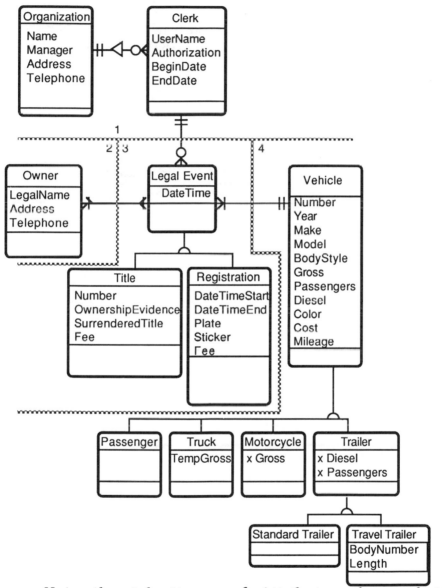

Note the inheritance of Attributes—the explicit representation of commonality—within the two Classification

Structures, "Legal Event" and "Vehicle." Also note the Attribute overrides in the "Vehicle" Classification Structure.

The Instance Connections portray the multiplicity and participation constraints of this particular registration and title system.

Example—Real-Time Airlift System

Subject Layer:

1. Mission ◀—▶ 2. Aircraft ◀—▶ 3. Radar

Attribute Layer:

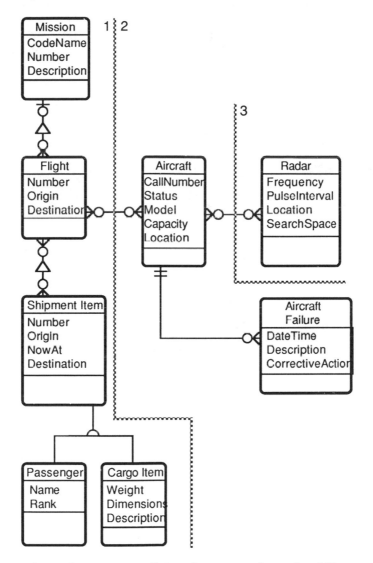

Note the inheritance of Attributes within the "Shipment Item" Classification Structure.

The Instance Connection between "Radar" and "Aircraft" applies in a problem space with multiple aircraft, and the need to be able to know which radar's data was used in determining the position of an aircraft. The key point here is that the multiplicity and participation constraints are set by an interpretation of the problem space; the interpretation must then be verified by problem space experts, with the client, or both.

A.6 DEFINING SERVICES

Notation

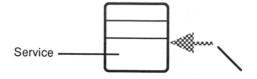

Service

Message Connection

specification <Object name>

> **descriptiveAttribute** <...>
> **definitionData** <...>
> **alwaysDerivableAttribute** <...>
> **occasionallyDerivableAttribute** <...>
>
> **externalSystemInput** <...>
> **externalSystemOutput** <...>
>
> **instanceConnectionConstraint** <...>
>
> **stateEventResponse** <...>
> **objectLifeHistory** <...>
>
> **notes** <...>
>
> **service** <...>
>
> **service** <...>
>
> **service** <...>
>
> **end specification**

Strategy

Service = the processing to be performed upon receipt of a message.

Identify Services. Primary strategy: fundamental Services—"Occur" (add, change, delete, and select), "Calculate," and "Monitor." Secondary strategy #1: Object life history—define the basic sequence, check for variations in each step, the add steps; finally, add Services. Secondary strategy # 2: State-Event-Response—define the major system states, list the external events and required responses, expand the Services and Message Connections.

Identify Message Connections; add Message Connections for instances already connected by Instance Connections; then, examine processing needed by one instance from another, looking for additional Message Connections.

Specify the Services: focus on the required externally observable behavior; use a template; add diagrams to simplify the specifications; develop narratives; and put the documentation set together.

Example—Sensor

Service Layer:

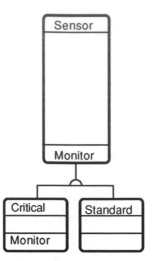

Note the inheritance in the "Sensor" Classification Structure. Sensor.Monitor is defined for all sensors, explicitly capturing processing commonality. The processing is then specialized by Critical.Monitor. Also observe that no additional Attributes or processing are needed for standard sensors.

Example—Registration and Title

Subject Layer:

Service Layer:

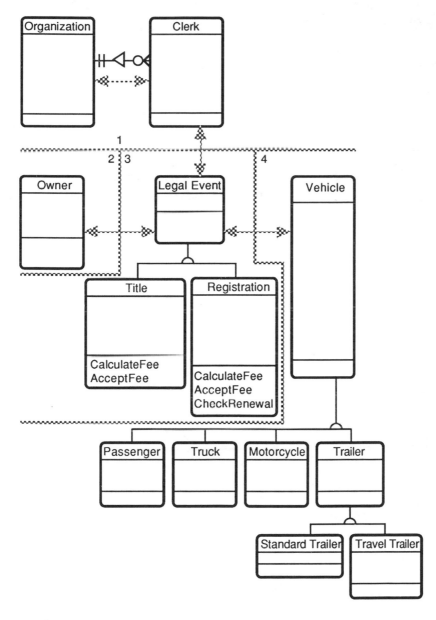

The Services "CalculateFee" and "AcceptFee" are entirely different. So, no generalization of these Services is shown within "LegalEvent."

"Registration.CheckRenewal" checks for registrations nearing expiration to issue renewal notices.

Example—Real-Time Airlift System

Subject Layer:

```
┌──────────┐        ┌───────────┐        ┌──────────┐
│1. Mission│◄══─══► │2. Aircraft│◄══─══► │3. Radar  │
└──────────┘        └───────────┘        └──────────┘
```

Service Layer:

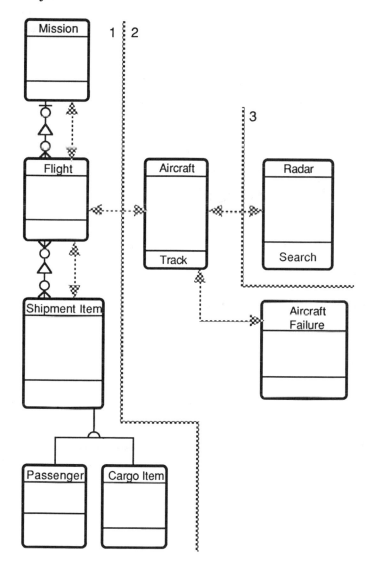

Appendix B

MAPPING OOA TO DOD-STD-2167A

B.1 DOD-STD-2167A

DOD-STD-2167A, *Defense System Software Development*, establishes a standard for planning and controlling software development on large software development projects. The standard is primarily used within the United States (e.g., Department of Transportation, Department of Defense). Some countries outside the USA use the standard too, generally for work under contract with a US firm developing a system in that country.

US industry and Government personnel worked for several years to establish a uniform standard for large software development projects. One of the authors advised on the practical application of software methods and the standard even while the standard was in draft form. The US Government released an initial version of the standard, DOD-STD-2167 on June 4, 1985.

A number of invitation-only workshops continued (one of the authors was actively involved in this review and refinement process). Many changes were needed, based upon application of the standard. The outcome was the publication of a shorter (!), simpler (!!) standard, DOD-STD-2167A, on February 29, 1988.

B.2 BENEFITS: POINT/COUNTERPOINT

2167A has certain benefits for the Government: visibility and control, plus a consistent framework. But before applying the standard, let alone using OOA with it, consider the arguments for and against these benefits—which are presented below in a "point/counterpoint" approach.

Consider the issue of visibility and control. *Point.* The message from the Government to the contractor is simple: cost overruns and schedule setbacks are not acceptable. We want more visibility into what you are doing, and we want you to exert more control over your software development process. Moreover, we want documented systems. *Counterpoint.* Too much time and too much money are the drawbacks. Estimates of the cost of fulfilling 2167A requirements range from 30 to 55 percent of overall cost (see "Paper: the Parent of Perfidious Practices," *Defense Science*, July 1988, p. 60), and talent is consumed fulfilling the letter of the 2167A law. Document-driven engineering (engineering dominated by filling out sections of a document) is all too weak engineering. Documented systems are vital for helping a maintenance staff understand an overall system during ongoing system maintenance. But, traditionally, no maintainer worth his salt has relied ultimately on anything but the code; even in-line comments are considered suspect by experienced maintainers. Volumes of unread paper won't help solve the expense of continuing engineering.

Consider instead a consistent framework. *Point.* 2167A provides a consistent framework for software development. Such a framework makes it easier for us to assess progress on the many contracts we are responsible for. And such consistency will eventually help us develop project-level metrics, so we improve the planning and controlling of future projects. *Counterpoint.* Consistency perhaps, but at what expense—taxpayer dollars for river rafts (volume after volume of documentation)? And, who is the audience (to use just one example) of a five-foot stack of requirements specifications? The technical staff? No—documents are shipped unread by the technical director (it's simply too much paper). The Government reviewer? No—many times the reviewer's job is to find a maximum number of defects in a very limited time (e.g., 2-4 weeks). So reviewers focus on format and inter-book consistency (referred to as a Sesame Street check...one of these things is not like the other, one of these things is not the same) rather than on content. A better alternative is a consistent framework applied to a high-level 100 page summary, plus a package of engineering products for those few reviewers who have the time and desire to examine the details further.

So, visibility and control plus a consistent framework are desirable. But to actually achieve these ends takes much more than cranking through a project following the letter of the 2167A law. It takes conscientious, continual effort by both the Government and contractor to ensure that useful, readable, and read documentation is produced; the documents must be streamlined and focused at specific readers to achieve specific results.

B.3 KEY IMPROVEMENTS WITH 2167A

Two additional 2167A benefits are actually improvements made over the earlier 2167 standard. These benefits are development cycle independence and software method independence.

B.3.1   Development Cycle Independence

The earlier 2167 standard presented the classical "waterfall" model for the development cycle—analysis, preliminary design, detailed design, code and unit test, and so forth. 2167 strongly reflects this phase-by-phase approach to soft-ware development. Because most Government systems to date had followed that pattern, it seemed reasonable to cap-ture the state of the practice. In contrast, 2167A goes to great pains to avoid even suggesting a development cycle. Rather than use the term "phase" (smacking of a waterfall approach), 2167A uses the term "activity." The contractor defines how to organize activities over time, and includes the description in the Software Development Plan. This lack of

Government direction means that the contractor can select his process model—waterfall, rapid prototype, multiple build, spiral, or some hybrid of these. Of course, the selection must be agreed upon by the Government. Once approved, the software development process is established for that contract (modifiable only through agreed-upon revisions to the Software Development Plan).

B.3.2   Software Method Independence

2167 attempted to remain "method independent" and at the same time prescribe some "default methods" that reflected the state of the practice. In applying the standard, the Government and contractor stuck with the default—it seemed the safe thing to do. Yet this default was not the intent of the standard.   2167A again goes to great lengths to avoid suggesting a default or what might be a minimum state of the practice requirement. For example, the major sections of a Software Requirements Specification are no longer broken up into "Functions" (implying a functional decomposition is required), but rather into "Capabilities." The contractor defines what constitutes a capability (e.g., for OOA a Capability may be an Object or collection of Objects) and includes it in the Software Development Plan. This level of independence means that the contractor can select his software methods (e.g., OOA or some in-house version of OOA for requirements analysis). Yes, the selection must be agreed-upon by the Government. And yes, once approved, the software development process is established for that contract (modifiable only through agreed-upon revisions to the Software Development Plan).

These two—development cycle independence and software method independence—are welcome improvements to the standard.

B.4 2167A FOR COMMERCIAL SYSTEMS?

The simple answer to this question is *not a chance*. Visibility and control, plus the concept of a consistent framework, can be achieved with simpler standards and less cost.

Yes, 2167A can be consulted to see what content might be appropriate in your organization. Just remember to consider the cost versus benefit every step along the way. And consider how much of your development dollar you are willing to spend on documents. Be sure it is money well spent.

B.5 OOA AND 2167A DOCUMENTATION: AN OVERVIEW

OOA is directly applicable during the system engineering and software requirements analysis activities of 2167A. The remainder of this chapter presents documents of interest in the application of OOA:

For the System Engineer:

System/Segment Specification.
System/Segment Design Document.

For Software Engineering Management:

Software Development Plan.

For the Software Requirements Engineer:

Software Requirements Specification(s).
Interface Requirements Specification.

B.6 SYSTEM/SEGMENT SPECIFICATION (SSS)

The System/Segment Specification (SSS) describes the requirements of a system or a segment of a system.

The SSS outline is:

1	**Scope.**
2	**Applicable Documents.**
3	**System Requirements.**
4	**Quality Assurance Provisions.**
5	**Preparation for Delivery.**
6	**Notes.**
10, 20, ...	**Appendixes.**

System engineers can apply OOA to develop engineering results for the paragraphs presented in the following:

3.1 Definition.

This paragraph provides a brief description of the system. So include "system diagram" (referred to in this document's Data Item Description) and a Subject layer, along with text to give a succinct overview of the system.

3.2.1 Performance Characteristics.

This section summarizes the system's capabilities in the context of the states in which the system can exist and the modes of operation within each state.

3.2.1.X (State Name).

This paragraph identifies and briefly describes a system state.

3.2.1.X.Y (Mode Name).

This paragraph identifies a mode of operation within a defined state.

3.2.1.X.Y.Z (System Capability Name and Project-Unique Identifier).

This paragraph specifies a capability, its purpose, and its parameters.

3.2.2 System Capability Relationships.

Map the results from OOA into this section. From the OOA Repository, use the processing requirements, service parameters, and state-dependent information about each Service. Use State-Event-Response Table(s) from the OOA Repository to help construct this section.

A table can be especially helpful in presenting this state-mode-capability summary.

3.2.3 External Interface Requirements.

3.2.3.X (System Name) External Interface Description.

This paragraph describes the requirements for interfaces with other systems. Detailed interface descriptions are defined in referenced documents.

For each Object that corresponds to an external system, include the external inputs and outputs from the OOA Repository in this section.

B.7 SYSTEM/SEGMENT DESIGN DOCUMENT (SSDD)

The System/Segment Design Document (SSDD) specifies the design of a system/segment and its operational and support environments. The SSDD outline is:

```
1        Scope.
2        Applicable Documents.
3        Operational Concepts.
4        System Design.
5        Processing Resources.
6        Quality Factor Compliance.
7        Requirements Traceability.
8        Notes.
10, 20, ... Appendixes.
```

System engineers can apply OOA to develop engineering results for the paragraphs presented in the following:

3.4 System Architecture.

This paragraph describes the internal structure of the system, in terms of segments (sub-systems), Hardware Configuration Items (HWCIs), and Computer Software Configuration Items (CSCIs). It identifies the purpose of and the relationships between components. It also identifies and gives the purpose of external interfaces (external to the system). A "system architecture diagram" (referred to in this document's Data Item Description) may be included.

CSCI selection can have a very significant impact on software development cost.

n CSCIs ==>
   n Software Requirements Specifications
   n Software Design Documents (Preliminary Design)
   n Software Design Documents (Detailed Design)
   n Software Test Documents.

A CSCI is an arbitrary chunk of software used for configuration management and control.

As a requirements engineer, take these factors into consideration when choosing CSCIs:

1. Don't pattern the CSCIs after the hardware architecture.

2. Check the tools and procedures for multi-volume documentation development and production.

3. Identify CSCIs in such a way that Objects are not split or duplicated into different CSCIs.

First, a CSCI should not be a reflection of the HWCI architecture. Hardware engineers often seem to think this idea is good; fight them! One reason to avoid using the architecture is its extreme volatility; someday the architecture that was promised to "never, ever, ever change" *will* change, at a disastrous documentation cost. Also, using hardware architecture ignores the fact that more than one piece of hardware may have common software requirements, or ones that are very similar (best represented with a Classification Structure).

Second, consider the question of tools. 2167A book production often involves a good deal of "boiler plate" text. Sections 1 and 2 plus the higher level components of other sections tend to drone on. Do you have the documentation tools and procedures to facilitate writing and maintaining a single copy of such material? And do the tools support inter-book consistency checking or just intra-book consistency checking?

If you don't have the support you need, compare the cost of a single or a few CSCIs versus several dozen. Keep the number of CSCIs down; one CSCI may be quite appropriate.

Third, when multiple CSCIs are desired, select the CSCIs based upon groupings of Subjects, Structures, and Objects. Your motivation for this choice is to minimize the interfaces between CSCI volumes, and eliminate requirements redundancy across volumes.

3.5 Operational Scenarios.

This paragraph describes each operational scenario of the system. It identifies the Configuration Items (HWCIs and CSCIs) applicable by states and modes. It also presents the general flow of execution control and data between Configuration Items.

Use OOA to complete this section for the CSCIs you selected. Identify the operational scenarios. Then use the OOA Repository (its Service specifications and state-event response table(s)) to identify the state and mode applicability of the CSCIs you chose.

Use Message connections between Subject, Structures, and Objects in different CSCIs to identify and present the general flow of execution control and data between Configuration Items. Use a finite state machine to show the overall sequence dependencies between the selected CSCIs.

4	System Design.
4.1	HWCI Identification.
4.1.X	(HWCI Name and Project-Unique Identifier).
4.2	CSCI Identification.
4.2.X	(CSCI Name and Project-Unique Identifier).

This section identifies the HWCIs and CSCIs. For each CSCI, the section includes a statement of purpose, SSS requirements allocation, interfaces external to the system, interfaces internal to the system, and any design constraints.

Use Message connections between Subject, Structures, and Objects in different CSCIs to identify the interfaces.

4.4	Internal Interfaces.
4.4.1	(HWCI-to-HWCI).
4.4.2	(HWCI-to-CSCI).
4.4.3	(CSCI-to-CSCI).

This section depicts the interfaces internal to the system, showing the interfaces between the Configuration Items (HWCIs and CSCIs), including sender, receiver, and message content.

Again, use Message Connections between Subject, Structures, and Objects in different CSCIs, this time to identify the sender, receiver, and message content.

B.8 SOFTWARE DEVELOPMENT PLAN (SDP)

The Software Development Plan (SDP) describes the contractor's plans for conducting software development.

Keep the SDP at a high level. Use other documents to detail each section. This plan keeps the SDP less susceptible to change, and keeps the volume from becoming so large as to overwhelm the reader.

The SDP outline is:

1	Scope.
2	Referenced Documents.
3	Software Development Management.

4   Software Engineering.
5   Formal Qualification Testing.
6   Software Product Evaluations.
7   Software Configuration Management.
8   Other Software Development Functions.
9   Notes.
10, 20, ... Appendixes.

Include OOA in the following sections:

3.2   Schedules and Milestones.
3.2.1 Activities.
3.2.2 Activity Network.

These paragraphs briefly describe (in 3.2.1) the software development activities and corresponding schedule. The activity network (3.2.2) shows the sequential constraints among activities. Include the application of OOA in the schedule, with key milestones for versions of the OOA model (e.g., preliminary, draft, and final) and for versions of the Software Requirements Specification(s) and the Interface Requirements Specification.

4.1.3   Software Engineering Environment.

This section includes plans for establishing and maintaining the needed software engineering environment.

Include the hardware and software considerations for CASE tool support of OOA, plus support for document generation and production.

4.2.1   Software Development Techniques and Methodologies.

This paragraph identifies and describes the methods to be used for each software development activity. (Note: methodology is a study of methods. What this paragraph is asking for is methods. Just don't change the 2167A title of this paragraph—your document may be found to be non-compliant if you do!)

Identify and briefly describe the use of OOA during the Software Requirements Analysis activity. Also, state that each

SRS Capability corresponds to an Object or a collection of related Objects.

> **6.5** **Activity-Dependent Product Evaluations.**
> **6.5.X** **Software Product Evaluation—**
> **(activity name).**

This paragraph presents plans for conducting project evaluations. Evaluation criteria, procedures, and tools are identified.

Include the OOA checklist for early detection and correction of errors, inconsistencies, and unnecessary complexity. Keep the information at a high level; place the detailed checks into a short practitioner's crib sheet.

B.9 SOFTWARE REQUIREMENTS SPECIFICATION (SRS)

The Software Requirements Specification (SRS) specifies the engineering and qualification requirements for a Computer Software Configuration Item (CSCI). The SRS is used as the basis for design and formal testing of a CSCI.

The SRS outline is:

> 1 Scope.
> 2 Applicable Documents.
> 3 Engineering Requirements.
> 4 Qualification Requirements.
> 5 Preparation for Delivery.
> 6 Notes.
> 10, 20, ... Appendixes.

Include OOA in the following sections:

> **3.1 CSCI External Interface Requirements.**

This paragraph identifies and describes all interfaces external to the CSCI (meaning, with other CSCIs, with HWCIs, and with other systems).

Include the external inputs and outputs from the OOA Repository, plus the message interaction between users and the system. Also, include the Message Connections between CSCIs, when more than one CSCI is identified in the SSDD.

3.2 CSCI Capability Requirements.
3.2.X (Object Name and Project-Unique Identifier).

These paragraphs specify the capability requirements that the CSCI must satisfy. For 3.2, each capability and its states and modes must be summarized.

For 3.2.X, include an OOA diagram fragment for the Subject, Structure, or Object to be specified. Then include the corresponding Services specification from the repository.

3.3 CSCI Internal Interfaces.

This paragraph identifies the interfaces between the capabilities. Include the Message Connections between the capabilities.

3.4 CSCI Data Element Requirements.

This paragraph specifies the data elements for the CSCI (both the ones used in its external interfaces as well as the ones used internally).

Include the Attributes and external inputs and outputs from the OOA Repository, those which correspond to this CSCI. Be sure to include the required data constraints.

3.5 Adaptation Requirements.
3.5.1 Installation-Dependent Data.
3.5.2 Operational Parameters.

These paragraphs specify the requirements for adapting the CSCI to site-unique conditions and to changes in the environment. In 3.5.1, include the Attributes from "Site" Object(s). In 3.5.2, include the parameterized Attribute ranges, which can be set according to operational need.

3.9 Design Constraints.

This paragraph specifies requirements that constrain the CSCI design. Check the design notes folder that you compiled while building the OOA model. If a design constraint really must be levied from within the SRS, do it here.

B.10 INTERFACE REQUIREMENTS SPECIFICATION (IRS)

The Interface Requirements Specification (IRS) specifies the requirements for interfaces between CSCI(s) and other configuration or critical items.

The IRS outline is:

1	Scope.
2	Applicable Documents.
3	Interface Specification.
4	Quality Assurance.
5	Preparation for Delivery.
6	Notes.
10, 20, ...	Appendixes.

Include OOA results in the following paragraphs:

3.1	Interface Diagrams.
3.X	(Interface Name and Project-Unique Identifier).
3.X.1	Interface Requirements.
3.X.2	Data Requirements.

This section identifies the interfaces among CSCIs, HWCIs, and critical items to which the specification applies.

Include a "block diagram" (referred to by this document's Data Item Description) depicting the interfaces.

Include the external inputs and outputs from the OOA Repository plus the message interaction between the user and the system. Plus, include the Message Connections between CSCIs, when more than one CSCI is identified in the SSDD.

B.11   SUMMARY

You *can* follow good principles of analysis and design, and then figure out how to fit your results into the 2167A framework. Guard against letting the paperwork drive (and potentially overrun) the so very much needed strong engineering achievements.

BIBLIOGRAPHY

Primary Bibliography

1. Books

[Coad, 1989] Coad, Peter, *Object-Oriented Analysis.* Seminar notes. Object International (Austin, TX), 1989.

[Coad, 1989] Coad, Peter, *Object-Oriented DBMS.* Seminar notes. Object International (Austin, TX), 1989.

[Cox, 1986] Cox, Brad, *Object-Oriented Programming.* Addison-Wesley, 1986.

[Meyer, 1988] Meyer, Bertrand, *Object-Oriented Software Construction.* Prentice Hall, 1988.

[Shlaer and Mellor, 1988] Shlaer, Sally, and Mellor, Steve, *Object-Oriented Systems Analysis.* Prentice Hall, 1988.

[Smalltalk, 1986] *Smalltalk/V Tutorial and Handbook.* Digitalk, Inc., 1986.

2. Articles

[Conte, 1987] Conte, Paul "Understanding Relational Data Bases," *Computer Language,* May 1987.

[Danforth, 1988] Danforth, Scott, and Tomlinson, Chris, "Type Theories and Object-Oriented Programming," *A C M Computing Surveys,* March 1988.

[Hull and King, 1987] Hull, Richard and King, Roger, "Semantic Database Modeling: Survey, Applications, and Research Issues," *ACM Computing Surveys,* September 1987.

[Ladden, 1989] Ladden, Richard, "A Survey of Issues to be Considered in the Development of an Object-Oriented

217

Development Methodology for Ada," *Ada Letters,* March/April 1989.

[LBMS, 1987] "Entity Life Histories," Learmonth Burchett Management Systems, Houston and London, 1987.

[Loomis, Shaw, and Rumbaugh, 1987] Loomis, M., Shah, A., and Rumbaugh, J., "An Object Modeling Technique for Conceptual Design," *European Conference on OOP,* June 1987.

[Rumbaugh, 1988a] Rumbaugh, J., "Relational Database Design Using An Object-Oriented Methodology," *Communications of the ACM,* April 1988.

[Rumbaugh, 1987] Rumbaugh, J., "Relations as Semantic Constructs in an Object-Oriented Language," *ACM OOPSLA '87 Proceedings,* October 1987.

[Seidewitz and Stark, 1987] Seidewitz, Ed and Stark, Mike, "Towards a General Object-Oriented Software Development Methodology," *Ada Letters,* Volume 7, Number 4.

[Stankovic, 1988] Stankovic, John, "Misconceptions About Real-Time Computing," *IEEE Computer,* October 1988.

[Teorey, 1986] Teorey, T., Yang, D., and Fry, J., "A Logical Design Methodology for Relational Databases Using the Extended Entity-Relationship Model," *ACM Computing Surveys,* June 1986.

[Thomas, 1989] Thomas, Dave, "What's an Object?," *Byte,* March 1989.

Secondary Bibliography

1.   Books

[Berryman, 1984] Berryman, Gregg, *Notes on Graphic Design and Visual Communication.* William Kaufmann, 1984.

[Britannica] "Animal Behaviour," "Classification Theory," "Mood," *Encyclopedia Britannica.*

[Date, 1986] Date, C.J., *An Introduction to Database Systems.* Addison-Wesley, 1986.

[DeMarco, 1978] DeMarco, Tom, *Structured Analysis and System Specification.* Yourdon Press/Prentice Hall, 1978.

[Fisher, 1989] Fisher, Alan S., *CASE: Using Software Development Tools.* John Wiley & Sons, 1988.

[Gane and Sarson, 1979] Gane, Chris and Sarson, Trish, *Structured Systems Analysis: Tools and Techniques.* Prentice Hall, 1979.

[IEEE, 1983] *IEEE Standard Glossary of Software Engineering Terminology* (Standard 729). IEEE, 1983.

[Lanham, 1981] Lanham, Richard A., *Revising Business Prose.* Charles Scribner's Sons, 1981.

[McClure, 1989], McClure, Carma, *CASE Is Software Automation.* Prentice Hall, 1989.

[McMenamin and Palmer, 1984] McMenamin, Steve and Palmer, John, *Essential Systems Analysis.* Yourdon Press/Prentice Hall, 1984.

[Oxford, 1986] *Dictionary of Computing.* Oxford University Press, 1986.

[Page-Jones, 1988] Page-Jones, Meilir, *The Practical Guide to Structured Systems Design.* 2nd edition, Yourdon Press/Prentice Hall, 1988.

[Rosenau, 1981] Rosenau, Milton, *Successful Project Management.* Wadsworth, 1981.

[Shertzer, 1986] Shertzer, Margaret, *The Elements of Grammar.* Macmillan, 1986.

[Strunk and White, 1979] Strunk Jr., W., and White, E. B., *The Elements of Style.* Macmillan, 1979.

[Yourdon, 1989] Yourdon, Edward, *Modern Structured Analysis.* Yourdon Press/Prentice Hall, 1989.

[Yourdon and Constantine, 1979] Yourdon, Edward and Constantine, Larry, *Structured Design.* Prentice Hall, 1979.

2. Articles

[Apple, 1989a] "The Future Belongs to OOP," *Apple Viewpoints,* December 19, 1988.

[Apple, 1989b] "The Power of Object-Oriented Programming," *Apple Direct,* February 1989.

[Boehm, 1988] Boehm, Barry, "Understanding and Controlling Software Costs," *IEEE Transactions on Software Engineering,* October 1988.

[Booch, 1986] Booch, Grady, "Object-Oriented Development," *IEEE Transactions on Software Engineering,* February 1986.

[Bruce, 1988] Bruce, Thomas, "CASE Brought Down to Earth," *Database & Programming Design,* October 1988.

[Chen, 1988] Chen, C. William, "The DBA's Changing Role," *Database Design & Programming,* October 1988.

[Fischer, 1989] Fischer, Gerhard, "Human-Computer Interaction in Software: Lessons Learned, Challenges Ahead," *IEEE Software,* January 1989.

[Ingalls, 1981] Ingalls, David, "Design Principles Behind Smalltalk," *Byte,* August 1981.

[Jacobsen, 1987] Jacobsen, Ivar, "Object-Oriented Development in an Industrial Environment," *ACM OOPSLA '87 Proceedings,* October 1987.

[Jalote, 1989] Jalote, Pankaj, "Functional Refinement and Nested Objects for Object-Oriented Design," *IEEE Transactions on Software Engineering*, March 1989.

[Kim, Ballou, Chou, Garza, and Woelk, 1988] Kim, Ballou, Chou, Garza, Woelk, "Integrating an Object-Oriented Programming System with a Database System," *ACM OOPSLA '88 Proceedings*, October 1988.

[Ladden, 1988] Ladden, Richard, "A Survey of Issues ... Object-Oriented ... and Ada," *ACM Software Engineering Notes*, July 1988.

[Lee, Rissman, D'Ippolito, Plinta, and Scoy, 1987] Lee, Rissman, D'Ippolito, Plinta, Scoy, "An OOD Paradigm for Flight Simulators," *CMU-SEI Technical Report*, December 1987.

[Lieberman, 1988] Lieberman, Daniel, "Codd's 12 Rules: A Method for DBMS Evaluation," *Database Programming and Design*, December 1988.

[Millikin, 1989] Millikin, Michael, "Object-Orientation: What It Can Do for You," *Computerworld*, March 13, 1989.

[Parnas, 1972] Parnas, David, "On the Criteria for Decomposing Programs into Modules," *Communications of the ACM*, December 1972.

[Potter and Trueblood, 1988] Potter, William and Trueblood, Robert, "Traditional, Semantic, and Hyper-Semantic Approaches to Data Modeling," *IEEE Computer*, June 1988.

[Ramamoorthy, 1988] Ramamoorthy, C.V., and Sheu, Phillip, "Object-Oriented Systems," *IEEE Expert*, Fall 1988.

[Rumbaugh, 1988b] Rumbaugh, Ed, "Controlling Propagation of Operations using Attributes on Relations," *ACM OOPSLA '88 Proceedings*, October 1988.

[Sanden, 1989a] Sanden, Bo, "An Entity-Life Modeling Approach to the Design of Concurrent Software," *Communications of the ACM*, March 1989.

[Sanden, 1989b] "The Case for Eclectic Design of Real-Time Software," *IEEE Transactions on Software Engineering,* March 1989.

[Seidewitz, 1987] Seidewitz, Ed, "Object-Oriented Programming in Smalltalk and Ada," *ACM OOPSLA '87 Proceedings,* October 1987.

[Seidewitz, 1989] Seidewitz, Ed, "Notes on Object-Oriented Analysis and Specification," Unpublished Notes, December 1988.

[Smith 1988] Smith, Connie, "Applying Synthesis Principles to Create Responsive Software Systems," *IEEE Transactions on Software Engineering,* October 1988.

[Stroustrup, 1988a] Stroustrup, Bjarne, "What is Object-Oriented Programming?" *IEEE Software,* May 1988.
Also, [Stroustrup88b] "A Better C," *Byte,* August 1988.

[Wing and Nixon, 1989] Wing, J.M. and Nixon, M.R., "Extending Ina Jo with Temporal Logic," *IEEE Transactions on Software Engineering,* February 1989. (Ina Jo is a trademark of SDC, now a part of Unisys.)

[Wegner, 1987] Wegner, Peter, "Dimensions of Object-Based Language Design," *ACM OOPSLA '87 Proceedings,* October 1987.

3.   Standards

[2167A] *DOD–STD–2167A, Defense System Software Development.* U.S. Department of Defense, February 29, 1988. To request a copy of 2167A and its Data Item Descriptions, write Naval Publications and Forms Center, 5801 Tabor Ave., Philadelphia PA 19120 USA. (In the U.S., copies may be requested by calling 215-697-2000).

4.   On-Line Forums

BIX, OOD Conference.

CompuServe, Computer Language Forum

INDEX

NOTES

NOTES

NOTES

NOTES

NOTES